The Heritage Book 1994

Edna McCann

Maxwell Macmillan Canada

Maxwell Macmillan Canada
1200 Eglinton Avenue East, Suite 200
Don Mills, Ontario M3C 3N1

ISBN 02.954183-2

Printed and bound in Canada
♾ Printed on Acid Free Paper

Eighteenth Edition

I CAN hardly believe that another year has passed since I last wrote an introduction to this little book. If anyone had told me when I wrote the first edition of *The Heritage Book* that I would be writing it for eighteen years I never would have believed it.

I first started collecting little stories and maxims after I heard a moving story about a man whose wife was very ill. The man knew that without his company she would be unhappy and would take longer to recover. Unfortunately, due to the nature of his job, he had to be constantly on the road.

One day the woman received a large parcel labeled "Medicine." Inside the box were many plastic capsules with the prescription to take one each morning and one before retiring. Inside each capsule was a funny memory that the couple cherished. In no time she got better.

So to my thousands of friends who read me every day I give you a year's supply of medicine. May God grant you happiness, good health, and peace throughout 1994.

Edna McCann

January

OLD One, lie down,
Your journey is done,
Little New Year
Will rise with the sun.
Now you have come to
The foot of the hill,
Lay down your bones,
Old Year, and lie still.

Young One, step out,
Your journey's begun,
Weary Old Year
Makes way for his son.
Now you have started
To climb up the hill,
Put best foot forward,
New Year, with a will.

—*Eleanor Farjeon*

THE HERITAGE BOOK

So teach us to number our days, that we may apply our hearts into wisdom.

—Psalm 90: 12

Now that the hustle and bustle of the holiday season has passed it is time, once again, to pack away the festive decorations for another year.

Some people find this to be an onerous task but I, for one, really enjoy the last look at our Christmas treasures as I put them in their boxes. It seems that each ornament, wreath or candle has its own special memory. As I wrap each item in tissue I have a chance to think about how long we've had it, the circumstances of our getting it, and who gave it to us. All of these things are beautiful memories that I have a chance to enjoy each Christmas season.

THE HERITAGE BOOK

Of all the lovely Christmas gifts that I receive I confess that my favourites are usually books. For an insatiable reader like me, a new book is like manna from heaven.

My dear friend Jake Frampton owns a book store and to my delight he always indulges me with several "hot off the press" new books each Christmas. This year was no exception.

Although I enjoy many types of literature I really love getting into a good mystery. Over the past few years some of my favourite authors have been Dick Francis, Queen Elizabeth's jockey who writes stories of the world of horse racing; Tom Clancy, whose stories of political intrigue are fascinating; and Len Deighton, whose hero's exploits move from book to book allowing the tension and suspense to build over much longer periods of time.

Once begun, I have a great deal of difficulty putting a book down. So I have devised a "reward" system for myself, and it works very well. I allow one chapter for making my bed, two chapters when the dishes are done, one for dusting, etc. It seems to be the only way to keep the house tidy.

THE HERITAGE BOOK

BERNIE S. Siegal, M.D., writes, "I've done research, and I hate to tell you, but everybody dies—lovers, joggers, vegetarians, and nonsmokers. I'm telling you this so that some of you who jog at 5 a.m. and eat vegetables will occasionally sleep late and have an ice cream cone."

I HAVE chosen the first verse of a hymn by Reverend Godfrey Thring to remind you that today is the celebration of the Epiphany.

From the Eastern mountains
Pressing on they came,
Wise men in their wisdom,
To His humble home;
Stirred by deep devotion,
Hasting from afar,
Ever journeying onward,
Guided by a star.
Light of Light that shineth
Ere the worlds began,
Draw Thou near and lighten
Every heart of man.

THE HERITAGE BOOK

FRIDAY — JANUARY 7

THE art of acceptance is the art of making someone who has just done you a small favour wish that he or she might have done you a greater one.

SATURDAY — JANUARY 8

HAVE you ever noticed that people who tell us something for our own good never seem to have anything good to tell us?

SUNDAY — JANUARY 9

O LORD, we beseech thee mercifully to receive the prayers of thy people which call upon thee; and grant that they may both perceive and know what things they ought to do, and also may have grace and power faithfully to fulfil the same; through Jesus Christ our Lord. Amen.

—Collect for the first Sunday after the Epiphany, from The Book of Common Prayer.

THE HERITAGE BOOK

Announced by all the trumpets of the sky
Arrives the snow, and driving o'er the fields
Seems nowhere to alight; the whited air
Hides hills and woods, the river and the
    heaven,
And veils the farmhouse at the garden's end.

The sled and traveler stopped, the couriers
    feet
Delayed, all friends shut out, the
    housemates sit
Around the radiant fireplace, enclosed
In a tumultuous privacy of storm.
                        —*Ralph Waldo Emerson*

Many times a day I realize how much my
own outer and inner life is built upon the
labours of my fellow men, both living and
dead, and how earnestly I must exert myself in
order to give in return as much as I have received.

                        —*Albert Einstein*

THE HERITAGE BOOK

As any of you who have young children know, it can be difficult to raise children to be keenly competitive while teaching them that winning isn't everything. In a recent conversation with my great grandson Justin I have discovered that his parents, Phyllis and Bill, must be getting this lesson across.

Justin dropped in on his way home from school, and over cookies and hot chocolate we were discussing the events of the day.

"Guess what, Gran! The teacher picked me to be captain of one of the science "quiz kids" teams. I got to choose my team, and we won. We did AMAZING!"

When I asked Justin (who is very competitive) how he had picked his team-mates, his answer showed a sensitivity that surprised but pleased me greatly.

"Well Gran, I decided to pick the kids that nobody ever picks for anything, because I was thinking that it must not be much fun to NEVER get picked. Everybody thought I was dumb and they were sure we would lose. But we didn't. That's what's so great!"

THE HERITAGE BOOK

Thursday — January 13

An optimist is one who takes cold water thrown upon his idea, heats it with enthusiasm, and uses the steam to push ahead.

Friday — January 14

A man's worst enemy can't wish him what he thinks up for himself.

—Yiddish proverb

Saturday — January 15

Today is the birthdate of the late Martin Luther King Jr. In his honour, I offer this short verse, "Life and Death" by James Montgomery.

Beyond this vale of tears
There is a life above.
Unmeasured by the flight of years;
And all that life is love.

THE HERITAGE BOOK

SUNDAY — JANUARY 16

IF thou draw out thy soul to the hungry, and satisfy the afflicted soul, then shall thy light rise in obscurity, and thy darkness be as the noonday; and the Lord shall guide thee continually.

—Isaiah 58: 10-11

MONDAY — JANUARY 17

MUSIC, when soft voices die,
Vibrates in the memory—
Odours, when sweet violets sicken,
Live within the sense they quicken.

Rose leaves, when the rose is dead,
Are heaped for the beloved's bed;
And so thy thoughts, when thou art gone,
Love itself shall slumber on.

—Percy Bysshe Shelley

TUESDAY — JANUARY 18

GET someone else to blow your horn and the sound will carry twice as far.

—Will Rogers

THE HERITAGE BOOK

My sister Sarah and her husband Richard live on Canada's east coast. Over the years Sarah and I have kept in touch by frequent letters and lengthy phone conversations. My grandson Marshall has come up with an even better way to share the family news. We have made a videotape.

Marg, Bruce and I started the tape, showing the newly painted and papered kitchen. We told them our latest news before passing the tape to Phyllis and Bill. They filmed part of Justin and Jenny's hockey game, some of the fierce storm of a few weeks ago, and themselves dressed up for a formal outing.

Marshall and Jamie videoed many other of their family activities before passing the tape along to the other aunts, uncles, and cousins.

The end result was a lengthy edition of the "McCann Family News" which we bundled up and mailed to Sarah and Richard.

Their phone call this evening reflected their joy and excitement in seeing and "visiting with" the whole family. We hope they will send us a tape in return, and that this will become an ongoing tradition.

THE HERITAGE BOOK

Thursday — January 20

I was interested to read in a recent edition of a family magazine that the major cause of death and disability in young children is car-related accidents. When correctly used, car seats are about seventy percent effective in preventing death and serious injury, but approximately a third of all car seats are used incorrectly.

I bring up this point to remind parents and grandparents how important seat belts and car seats are for your children's safety. It is also essential to learn how to use these safety features properly if we are to keep these precious little people safe in our care.

Friday — January 21

Most quarrels, like muddy water, will clear if you don't keep stirring them up.

SATURDAY — JANUARY 22

THE old familiar sight of ours
   Took marvelous shapes; strange domes and
   towers.
Rose up where sty or corn-crib stood,
Or garden wall, or belt of wood;
A smooth white mound the brush-pile showed
A fenceless drift what once was road;
The bridle-post an old man sat
With loose-flung coat and high cocked hat;
The well-curb had a Chinese roof;
And even the long sweep, high aloof,
In its slant splendor, seemed to tell
Of Pisa's leaning miracle.

—John Greenleaf Whittier

SUNDAY — JANUARY 23

IF thou draw out thy soul to the hungry, and
satisfy the afflicted soul; then shall thy light
rise in obscurity, and thy darkness be as the
noonday; and the Lord shall guide thee continually.

—Isaiah 58: 10-11

THE HERITAGE BOOK

ALL those qualities that make a person what they are, or make one person different from another, form our character. Many people have written of character and today I offer just a few of these ideas.

Character is like a tree and reputation like its shadow. The shadow is what we think of it; the tree is the real thing.

—Abraham Lincoln

Character is what you are in the dark.

—Dwight L. Moody

The measure of a man's real character is what he would do if he knew he would never be found out.

—Thomas Macauley

If I take care of my character, my reputation will take care of itself.

—Dwight L. Moody

My neighbour and dear friend Lila MacGuiness has suffered greatly from arthritis. At her doctor's suggestion she has begun a program of aqua therapy at our nearby recreation centre. Because Lila was concerned about going on her own I readily consented to be her "pool pal." We use the pool during "Seniors Hour," a time when only those over 65 have access to the various pools and equipment areas.

Water is the ideal place to work out because it allows movement of affected areas without pressure or further injury. Water also stimulates blood circulation. For optimal success The Arthritis Foundation recommends that the water temperature be 84°-90°F. In our pool, the temperature is a constant 88°F.

Lila and I do a series of exercises suggested by her doctor. Although I am not an arthritis sufferer I am feeling the benefits of this program as well. Some of you may want to look into this excellent way to exercise during the long winter months.

THE HERITAGE BOOK

Wednesday — January 26

WHAT parents leave in their children is much more important than what they leave to them.

Thursday — January 27

I HOPE you enjoy Christina Rossetti's prayer as much as I do.

O Lord, who art our Guide even unto death, grant us, I pray Thee, grace to follow Thee whithersoever Thou goest. In little daily duties to which Thou callest us, bow down our wills to simple obedience, patience under pain or provocation, strict truthfulness of word and manner, humility, kindness; in great acts of duty or perfection, if Thou shouldest call us to them, uplift us to self-sacrifice, heroic courage, laying down of life for Thy truth's sake, or for a brother. Amen.

FRIDAY — JANUARY 28

Life is like a journey on a train,
With two fellow travellers at each
windowpane,
I may sit beside you all the journey through,
Or I may sit elsewhere, never knowing you.
But should fate mark me to sit by your side,
Let's be pleasant travellers—it's so short a
ride!

SATURDAY — JANUARY 29

Never close your lips to those to whom you
have opened your heart.
—Charles Dickens

SUNDAY — JANUARY 30

The Lord will hold thy right hand, saying
unto thee, Fear not; I will help thee.
—Isaiah 41: 13

THE HERITAGE BOOK

On this very cold, last day of the month, I offer you this recipe for a delicious tomato soup.

1 onion minced
1 tbsp of peanut oil
4 tbsps of butter
3 tbsps of flour
6 medium-sized tomatoes, peeled, drained, and chopped
2 medium-sized potatoes, peeled and chopped
4 cups boiling water
1 bouquet garni
salt, fresh ground black pepper

Cook the minced onion in the oil and 2 tbsps of the butter until it is soft and golden. Stir in the flour, cook the mixture until the flour is golden, and then add the potatoes, tomatoes, water and bouquet garni. Season with salt and pepper as desired. Simmer the soup for 30 minutes, remove the bouquet garni, stir in the remaining butter, and pour the soup into a heated tureen.

February

Winter

WHEN icicles hang by the wall,
    And Dick the shepherd blows his nail,
And Tom bears logs into the hall,
And milk comes frozen home in pail;
When blood is nipped, and ways be foul,
Then nightly sings the staring owl.
Tu-whit, to-who! a merry note,
While greasy Joan doth keel the pot.

When all aloud the wind doth blow,
And coughing drowns the parson's saw,
And birds sit brooding in the snow,
And Marian's nose looks red and raw,

When roasted crabs hiss in the bowl,
Then nightly sings the staring owl
Tu-whit, to-who! a merry note,
While greasy Joan doth keel the pot.
                —*William Shakespeare*

WEDNESDAY — FEBRUARY 2

FEBRUARY 2nd is the day when we find out whether or not we will face prolonged winter weather.

Groundhogs in Gobblers Knob, near Punxatawny, Pennsylvania, and in Wiarton, Ontario, are our "weather reporters."

When the animals leave their holes on this date they reportedly check to see if they can see their shadows. If the shadows are seen they will return to their underground homes for another six weeks of winter.

Of course, this is just for fun but many people look on these little creatures as true harbingers of spring.

THURSDAY — FEBRUARY 3

No matter how faulty the other person's memory may be, it improves tremendously when recalling your mistakes.

THE HERITAGE BOOK

<u>FRIDAY — FEBRUARY 4</u>

HAPPY the man, and happy he alone,
He who can call today his own;
He who, secure within, can say,
Tomorrow do your worst, for I have lived today.
—John Dryden

<u>SATURDAY — FEBRUARY 5</u>

COMMON sense is the most widely shared commodity in the world, for every man is convinced that he is well supplied with it.
—René Descartes

<u>SUNDAY — FEBRUARY 6</u>

SEARCH me, O God, and know my heart: try me, and know my thoughts: and see if there be any wicked way in me, and lead me in the way of the everlasting.
—Psalm 139: 23-24

THE HERITAGE BOOK

THIS past weekend we spent a most enjoyable day at my grandson Fred's home in the country.

Fred, his wife June, and his children Mickey and Geoffrey planned a winter picnic for us. What a feast it was!

The boys had built an enormous fire in a clearing at the back of the yard. I was given a place of honour on a padded lawn chair complete with a down-filled sleeping bag. I appreciated the extra warmth on a cold day.

June had prepared an enormous pot of baked beans which simmered over the fire. The boys roasted weiners for us all and Fred completed the meal with hot bread, wedges of cheddar cheese, and hot cider.

It was a glorious feeling to be able to enjoy some precious family time, a delicious meal, and a typical Canadian winter's day.

Any of you who have felt winter to be too long might well find a picnic such as we had to be a terrific "pick-me-up."

THE HERITAGE BOOK

SNOWFLAKES are one of nature's most fragile things, but just look at what they can do when they stick together.

FAMOUS last words: When the federal income tax was signed into law on October 3, 1913 in the United States, a senator speaking in opposition stated, "If we allow this one percent foot in the door, at some future date it might rise to five percent!"

STRIKE from mankind the principle of faith and men would have no more history than a flock of sheep.

—Edward G. Bulwer-Lytton

THE HERITAGE BOOK

THE hectic pace of our modern world often takes its toll, particularly on our young people.

Debbie, a neighbour and mother of three small children, expressed a common complaint during her visit today.

"Edna, my goal is to get caught up so that I can be on top of my life instead of buried underneath it. I feel overwhelmed."

Debbie and her husband have full-time jobs, three children, and a house to take care of. They each need some personal time as well as time shared as a couple. Often it is the accumulation of small things that is enervating— the pile of dirty laundry, the refrigerator that needs cleaning, mail that needs sorting.

Over the years I have found that taking action galvanizes the spirit. When you do even one thing you cut through that feeling of being overwhelmed, and new energy and vitality are unleashed.

Marg and I offered to take the children for a day so that Debbie and her husband can have a catch-up day together. Perhaps this will help a nice young couple clean up the outward turmoil and find time to enjoy their family, their home, and each other.

THE HERITAGE BOOK

MY good friends Will and Muriel came by today. The course of our conversation turned, as it often does, to our children and grandchildren. Muriel was telling me about her grandson John, who had been a nail-biter for many years. Many remedies had been tried, from bribes to painting bitter substances on his nails.

Will then explained how he had helped John finally break this troublesome habit.

"I read about this habit-breaker a few years ago. It's a psychological trick—when the urge to bite strikes, you just clench your fists for three minutes. I asked John to try it for a few weeks. Four weeks later his nails had grown significantly. He and his parents are really pleased with the results."

One of the joys of being a grandparent is being able to call upon our experience to help our loved ones.

THE HERITAGE BOOK

BUT the souls of the righteous are in the hand of God, and there shall no torment touch them. In the sight of the universe they seemed to die: and their departure is taken for misery, and their going from us to be utter destruction: but they are in peace.

—Wisdom of Solomon 3: 1-3

Valentine's Day

I DO not need a fancy heart
With Cupid's dart and bow,
To tell me in a flowery verse
What I already know.

I do not need a costly gift
Presented as a sign,
That though the years have come and gone
I'm still your valentine.

I only need your loving smile
Each time I look your way . . .
For this to be from start to end
A perfect Valentine's Day.

—Author unknown

TUESDAY — FEBRUARY 15

HAVE you noticed that as we get older, the days get longer but the years get shorter?

WEDNESDAY — FEBRUARY 16

Ash Wednesday

ALMIGHTY and everlasting God, who hatest nothing that thou hast made, and dost forgive the sins of all them that are penitent: Create and make in us new and contrite hearts, that we worthily lamenting our sins, and acknowledging our wretchedness, may obtain of thee, the God of all mercy, perfect remission and forgiveness; through Jesus Christ our Lord. Amen.

—Collect for Ash Wednesday
from The Book of Common Prayer

THURSDAY — FEBRUARY 17

WE are better able to study our neighbours than ourselves, and their actions than our own.

—Aristotle

THE HERITAGE BOOK

Even Such is Time

Even such is Time, that takes in trust
Our youth, our joys, our all we have,
And pays us but with earth and dust;
  Who in the dark and silent grave,
When we have wander'd all our ways,
Shuts up the story of our days;
But from this earth, this grave, this dust,
My God shall raise me up, I trust.

—Sir Walter Raleigh

Once uttered, words run faster than horses.

—Japanese proverb

THE HERITAGE BOOK

THEN Jesus was led up by the Spirit into the wilderness to be tempted by the devil. And after he had fasted forty days and forty nights, He then became hungry. And the tempter came and said to Him, "If you are the Son of God, command that these stones become bread." But he answered them and said "It is written, 'Man shall not live on bread alone, but on every word that proceeds out of the mouth of God.'"

A MAN may travel far in his life, but there is always a small part of him that never leaves the town where he was born, the neighbourhood where he spent his boyhood. Hometowns can be big or small, a hamlet hardly on the highway, or the neighbourhood of a large city. But large or small, a hometown holds the memories of youth.

—*D. Valentine*

THE HERITAGE BOOK

Marg, Bruce and I have been watching endless hours of television, something that is unusual for us. What has captured our attention, and the attention of millions around the world, is the coverage of the Winter Olympics from Lilliehammer, Norway.

It is interesting to note that only two years have passed since the last Winter Olympic games were held here in 1992. Usually there are four years between games, but for financial reasons this has been changed to a set of winter games two years apart, followed by a similar set of summer games. This means that the Summer Olympics will be held in 1996 and 1998. Following this the winter games will return to their four-year cycle.

I think the Olympic Games bring out something wonderful in all of us. Who could watch these marvellous young athletes compete and not say "They are the best! And they are Canadian!"

COURAGE is the strength that comes from within that allows us to master our fear when we confront danger, pain, or difficulty. I offer just a few thoughts on "courage" today.

He that loses wealth, loses much;
But he that loses courage, loses all.
—Cervantes

COWARDS die many times before their deaths; the valiant never taste of death but once.
—William Shakespeare

LIFE is mostly froth and bubble,
Two things stand like stone,
Kindness in another's trouble,
Courage in your own.
—Adam Lyndsay Gordon

YOU gain strength, courage, and confidence by every experience in which you really stop to look fear in the face. . . . You must do the thing you think you cannot do.
—Eleanor Roosevelt

THE HERITAGE BOOK

OF all the joys of childhood one of the most widely remembered, in North America at least, is the pursuit of the breakfast cereal premium.

The first Kellogg premium, which appeared in 1909, was modest: if you bought two boxes of Kellogg's Corn Flakes the counter man would hand you a "Funny Jungleland Moving Picture Book." The first true mail-away offer was made in 1925, again by Kellogg: for a dime and a box-top the sender received a set of printed cloth dolls.

Items were not actually placed in cereal boxes until 1943, when Pep put paper airplane cutouts in some packages.

Since then it has been an unstoppable deluge of diverse items, from baseball and hockey cards, stickers, 3D books and glasses, to iron-on T-shirt transfers and plastic Frisbees.

The most successful give-away was probably the miniature licence plates—some 50 million—given away by General Mills in 1953-54. But the most exciting premiums were Quaker Oats' deeds to a square inch of land in the Yukon, and Kelloggs' baking-powder powered atomic submarines for the bathtub.

How many can you remember?

THE HERITAGE BOOK

THERE are troubles that trouble the day
away;
There are troubles that wear our lives away;
But the troubles that trouble us most of all
Are the troubles that never happen at all.

—James S. Bach

WE can read poetry, and recite poetry, but
to live poetry is the symphony of life.

—S. Frances Foote

THESE things I have spoken unto you that in
me ye might have peace. In the world, ye
shall have tribulation: but be of good cheer, I
have overcome the world.

—John 16: 33

THE HERITAGE BOOK

My daughter Mary and her husband John joined us for dinner last evening. John is a minister and he knows how much I enjoy hearing stories from his parish. This is my favourite anecdote from last night.

John asked one little girl how she liked the singing of the congregation during that morning's service.

"I really liked it, but I don't think the rest of the people did."

"Why did you think that, Ashley?"

"Well, when the people were praying, I heard them say 'Lord have mercy on us miserable singers.'"

March

I WELCOME our new month with this poem by
Virginia K. Oliver.

It's the little things in life that count,
The things of every day;
Just the simple things that we can do,
The kind of words we say.
The little things like a friendly smile
For those who may be sad,
The clasp of a hand or kindly deed
To help make someone glad.
A knock on the door of lonely homes,
Or flowers bright and gay,
For someone to whom you might bring cheer
With just a small bouquet.
Just the little greetings here and there
On which so much depends,
The little pleasures that all can share,
The joy of making friends.

THE HERITAGE BOOK

<u>WEDNESDAY — MARCH 2</u>

F RIENDSHIP is the gift of the gods, and the most precious boon to man.

—Benjamin Disraeli

<u>THURSDAY — MARCH 3</u>

T HERE is only one success—to spend your life in your own way.

<u>FRIDAY — MARCH 4</u>

T HOSE who say all men are equal speak an undoubted truth, if they mean that all have an equal right to liberty, to their property, and to their protection of the laws. But they are mistaken if they think men are equal in their station and employments, since they are not so by their talents.

—Voltaire

THE HERITAGE BOOK

Amerian humorist Sam Revenson tells us of his life growing up a child of immigrant parents.

"I didn't know I had to 'feel like' doing my homework, practicing the violin, washing dishes or running errands. I just had to do it because everyone had to do things he really didn't feel like doing—even big people. I had a strong suspicion my father didn't feel like working twelve hours a day in a sweatshop."

Again the high priest was questioning Him, and saying to Him, "Are You the Christ, the Son of the Blessed One?" And Jesus said, "I am; and you shall see the Son of man sitting on the right hand of power and coming with the clouds of heaven." And tearing his clothes the high priest said "What further do we need of witnesses? You have heard the blasphemy; how does it seem to you?" And they all condemned Him to be deserving of death.

—Mark 14: 61-64

THE HERITAGE BOOK

As my former readers know, my grand-daughter Phyllis was a schoolteacher before she was married. She shared some of her views of today's educational system with me during her visit this past weekend.

"You know Gran, the catch phrase in education today is 'self-esteem.' We want children to feel good about themselves and to feel successful in their academic endeavours. It's my opinion though, that in many cases our children are being short-changed. If we accept work that is messy or poorly done with a pat on the head and a sticker aren't we encouraging mediocrity? If children think it is acceptable to do less than their best, what will make them want to do better? I think we underestimate our kids today. There are ways to tell a child 'You are terrific! But this work isn't—please give me your best!' without lowering their self-esteem. As well, I think that a return to teaching basic grammar, sentence parsing, etc. is essential."

I heartily agree.

THE HERITAGE BOOK

My grandson Marshall, a lawyer, has always been well-spoken and articulate. Maybe that is why he enjoys so much these malapropisms of the great moviemaker Sam Goldwyn.

A verbal contract isn't worth the paper it's written on.

I'll give you a definite maybe.

Include me out.

It's more than magnificent—it's mediocre.

A bachelor's life is no life for a single man.

We're overpaying him, but he's worth it.

Don't talk to me while I'm interrupting.

The scene is dull. Tell him to put more life into his dying.

THE HERITAGE BOOK

WEDNESDAY — MARCH 9

GROWING older confronts you with two great shocks. One is the first time they ask if you get the senior citizen discount. The other is the first time they don't ask if you get the senior citizen discount—they assume it.

THURSDAY — MARCH 10

IT is the first mild day of March.
Each minute sweeter than before.
The redbreast sings from the tall larch
That stands beside our door.

—William Wordsworth

FRIDAY — MARCH 11

IT doesn't take monumental feats to make the world a better place. It can be as simple as letting someone go ahead of us in a grocery line.

THE HERITAGE BOOK

No one to talk to, day by day,
The friends of youth are all away,
No one to lend a listening ear,
The twice-told tales to kindly hear.
No one to sit beside his chair
The gossip of the day to share;
For he is old and worn and white,
His youthful strength forgotten quite.

Once he was stalwart, strong and wise,
Ambition's fire within his eyes.
With honest hand and courage strong,
He stood for right against the wrong,
And labored hard with brawn and brain
A life's ambition to attain.
A kindly husband, father, friend,
The cause of right he would defend,
But now he's old and in the way,
With none to talk to all the day.
Oh, shame, that human hearts should spurn
The love for which the aged yearn!
How tenderly they need our care,
Our highest thought and aim to share!
Perhaps some time we'll be as they,
Feeble and worn and old and gray,
With none to talk to all the day.

—Helen B. Anderson

THE HERITAGE BOOK

"What man among you, if he has a hundred sheep and has lost one of them, does not leave the ninety-nine in the open pasture, and go after the one which is lost, until he finds it.

"And when he has found it, he lays it on his shoulders, rejoicing. And when he comes home, he calls together his friends and his neighbours, saying to them, 'Rejoice with me, for I have found my sheep which was lost!' I tell you that in the same way, there will be more joy in heaven over one sinner who repents, than over ninety-nine righteous persons who need no repentance."

—Luke 15: 4-7

I have not much patience with a thing of beauty that must be explained to be understood. If it does need added interpretation by someone other than the creator, then I question whether it has fulfilled its purpose.

—Charlie Chaplin

THE HERITAGE BOOK

TUESDAY — MARCH 15

Love makes those young whom age doth chill,
And whom he finds young, keeps young
still.

—William Cartwright

WEDNESDAY — MARCH 16

PRAYER is the doorbell on the gate of heaven.

THURSDAY — MARCH 17

St. Patrick's Day

MAY the road rise to meet you; may the
wind be always at your back, may the sun
shine warm upon your face. May the rain fall
soft upon your fields and until we meet again,
may God hold you in the palm of his hand.

—Old Irish proverb

THE HERITAGE BOOK

My friend Mavis Tewksbury is a longtime collector of miniature dollhouses. In her letter to me she described the miniature house that was presented to Queen Mary in 1924 from the people of England.

"It was designed by Sir Edwin Lutyens and constructed and furnished over a four-year period by many artists and craftsmen at a cost of one million dollars.

"Constructed in the Georgian style, it is 100 inches long, 62 inches deep, and three stories high. It sits on a base containing pull-out drawers packed with machinery to run the house. One drawer contains a formal garden which pops into bloom when pulled out.

"Hot and cold water flows out of silver taps into alabaster bathtubs; pastry ovens, fired by tiny pellets of coal, bake tiny crumpets in the kitchen; a tiny gramophone plays 'God save the King' in the nursery. In the library are hundreds of tiny handwritten books bound in leather. The wine cellar is stocked with miniature bottles of champagne, Madeira, and Bordeaux wines.

"This house is stored in Windsor Castle, Edna, and I would give my eyeteeth to be able to see it!"

THE HERITAGE BOOK

REFERENCE letters are always an important part of any student's application. Henry H. Hoffman, former admissions director of the University of Alabama Medical School, cited the following as one of the best that he ever received.

An old miner from a small town wrote, "Knowed this kid from the day he was born. He played with my kids, mowed my yard. I don't know if he has sense enough to make it in medical school, but I do know he'll be the kind of man I'd like to come here to take care of me and my folks."

AND Pilate was saying to them "Then what shall I do with Him whom you call King of the Jews?"

And they shouted back, "Crucify Him!"

But Pilate was saying to them, "Why, what evil has He done?" But they shouted all the more, "Crucify Him!"

—Mark 15: 12-14

MONDAY — MARCH 21

Two years ago today, my grandson Marshall and his wife Jamie gave our family a marvellous spring gift when their daughter Bethany was born. This delightful little girl has been a ray of sunshine for us all since that day. A pretty child, she has a wonderful temperament—always a smile on her tiny face—and she is content to be with others or to play quietly by herself.

Elton Trueblood said, "God has sent children into the world, not only to replenish it, but to serve as sacred reminders of something ineffably precious which we are always in danger of losing. The sacrament of childhood is thus a continuing revelation."

TUESDAY — MARCH 22

A smooth sea never made a skillful mariner; neither do uninterrupted prosperity and success qualify men for usefulness and happiness.

WEDNESDAY MARCH 23

READING makes a full man; meditation, a profound man; discourse, a clear man.

—Benjamin Franklin

THURSDAY — MARCH 24

THE hero is one who kindles a great light in the world, who sets up blazing torches in the dark streets of life for men to see by. The saint is the man who walks through the dark paths of the world, himself a light.

—Felix Adler

FRIDAY — MARCH 25

PRAYER is the very soul and essence of religion, and therefore prayer must be the very core of the life of man, for no man can live without religion.

—Mahatma Gandhi

THE HERITAGE BOOK

My daughter Julia recently returned from a business trip to Boston, and during her stay she visited "Aunt" Marcia, an old family friend.

"You know Aunt Marcia," she said at dinner this evening, "She insisted that I stay with her and was thrilled when I told her that I had a few extra days to spend sightseeing. She knows everything worth seeing in the city and we had a fabulous time together."

When we asked Julia what she most enjoyed she answered, "Oh that's easy. My favourite stop was the Boston Public Library. It is an architectural masterpiece and is the first publicly supported municipal library in the world. It contains more than five million books, more than one million manuscripts, some 253,000 rare books, plus children's books, musical scores, films, and patents on more than sixty-five miles of bookshelves. As well, the artwork is outstanding.

"My second favourite stop was 'Filene's Basement,' a wonderful place to shop for fashion bargains."

History and fashion—that's my daughter Julia!

THE HERITAGE BOOK

SUNDAY — MARCH 27

THEN the soldiers of the governor took Jesus into the Craetorium and gathered the whole Roman cohort around Him. And they stripped him and put a scarlet robe on Him. And after weaving a crown of thorns, they put it on His head, and a reed in His right hand; and they kneeled down before Him and mocked Him, saying, "Hail, King of the Jews!"

—Matthew 27: 27-30

MONDAY — MARCH 28

LEARN to listen. Opportunity sometimes knocks very softly.

TUESDAY — MARCH 29

OUR home joys are the most delightful earth affords, and the joy of parents in their children is the most holy joy of humanity. It makes their hearts pure and good, it lifts men up to their Father in heaven.

—Johann Pestolazzi

THE HERITAGE BOOK

IF we are strong, our character will speak for itself. If we are weak, words will be of no help.

—*John F. Kennedy*

I ENJOYED this little anecdote provided by our parish pastor.

When a minister heard a little boy use a profanity, he said "Son, every time I hear you swear, a cold chill runs down my spine."

"Wow!" said the boy, "If you had been at our house yesterday when Dad caught his finger in the door, you'd have frozen to death."

April

Good Friday

AND when the sixth hour had come, darkness fell over the whole land until the ninth hour. And at the ninth hour Jesus cried out with a loud voice, "Eloi, Eloi, Lama, Sabachthani?" which is translated "My God, my God, why has Thou forsaken me?"

And when some of the bystanders heard it, they began saying, "Behold, He is calling for Elijah."

And someone ran and filled a sponge with sour wine, put it on a reed, and gave Him a drink, saying "Let us see whether Elijah will come to take Him down."

And Jesus uttered a loud cry, and breathed His last.

—Mark 15: 33-37

THE HERITAGE BOOK

THE longer I live, the more satisfied I am of two things: first, that the truest lives are those that are cut rose-diamond fashion, with many facets answering to the many-planned aspects of the world about them; secondly, that society is always trying in some way or other to grind us down to a single flat surface. It is hard work to resist the grinding-down action.

—*Oliver Wendell Holmes*

Easter Sunday

THE great Easter truth is not that we are to live newly after death—that is not the great thing—but that we are to be new here and now by the power of the resurrection; not so much that we are to live forever as that we are to, and may, live nobly now because we are to live forever.

—*Phillips Brooks*

<u>MONDAY — APRIL 4</u>

WHEN a man is born in Ireland,
   sure the men that are so wise,
Gather round and sprinkle wisdom
   in the little fellow's eyes;
And they give him power to do a
   thing no other race can do,
For his eyes can tell a false friend
   from a real friend who is true.

When a man is born in Ireland,
   sure the wits all leave their graves,
And they gather round his cradle
   and become his willing slaves;
And the angels sing an anthem as
   the soul goes down to earth;
For they know the Lord just loves
   to hear about an Irish birth.

O lucky sons of Ireland, you are
   blessed beyond compare,
Whether Wit or Wisdom yields,
   in that you're sure to share;
The saving sense of humour makes
   an Irishman elate,
He'll pass a joke with Fortune, or
   he'll throw a kiss to Fate.

THE HERITAGE BOOK

TUESDAY — APRIL 5

BE brave. Even if you're not, pretend to be. No one can tell the difference.

WEDNESDAY — APRIL 6

NEVER deprive someone of hope; it might be all they have.

THURSDAY — APRIL 7

WHEN I was young, I admired clever people. Now that I am old, I admire kind people.

—Abraham Joshua Heschel

FRIDAY — APRIL 8

IF you have a garden and a library, you have everything you need.

—Cicero

THE HERITAGE BOOK

Saturday — April 9

Isn't it funny that so many of us get the urge to clean at this time of year? My son-in-law Bruce feels that this need follows a pattern of nature—birds and animals make nests or clean dens and burrows for the arrival of their new offspring. Farmers clean the land of winter debris to make way for new planting of seeds and the arrival of spring growth.

"Husbands," Bruce claims, "clean out old junk, (and sometimes old furniture) because sure as shootin' their wives will get the urge to clean their 'nests' and redo paint and wallpaper, and recover furniture. If we didn't get rid of some of the old stuff, we'd be buried alive in just a few short years."

I pondered his theory as I packed Marg's old papers and magazines for the dump.

Sunday — April 10

I have set before you life and death. . . . So choose life.

—Deuteronomy 30:19

THE HERITAGE BOOK

Many years ago my husband George and I visited our good friends Emily and Harry at their home in Vermont. It was just about this time of year and the snow was newly departed from the area.

Emily and Harry had sent detailed directions to their farm house and we enjoyed the scenery as we drove on the backroads of this beautiful state.

In due course we arrived at their driveway, a long and rather winding "trail" down to a magnificent and stately old house.

As we pulled into the driveway and headed downhill it became apparent that the road was a sea of slippery muck. George made a valiant effort to keep us on track, but to no avail. We sailed merrily down until our old car plowed doggedly to rest three feet into their porch at the front door.

Emily, with a Vermonter's dry wit, called gaily as she came out the door, "Oh look Harry, Edna and George have arrived!"

My grandson Marshall enjoys humorous signs and notices. These are just a few that he felt his Uncle John, a minister, might enjoy.

In front of St. James Anglican Church on Highway 4 at Neepawa, Manitoba:

> Drive carefully.
> You might hit
> An Anglican

Outside a church in Toronto:

> Work for the Lord
> The pay isn't much
> But the retirement benefits
> Are out of this world

Outside a church in Sudbury, Ontario, nearly demolished by a tornado:

> Praise the Lord, anyway!

As well—

> Church property
> Dumpeth Not!

> Keep Off
> This Means Thou

THE HERITAGE BOOK

RISK is essential. There is no growth or inspiration in staying within what is safe and comfortable. Once you find out what you do best, why not try something else?

—Alex Noble

A MAN leaves all kinds of footprints when he walks through life. Some you can see, like his children, and his house. Others are invisible, like the prints he leaves across other people's lives, the help he has given them and what he has said—his jokes, gossip that has hurt others, encouragement.

A man doesn't think about it but everywhere he passes, he leaves some kind of mark. All these marks added together are what man means.

—Margaret Lee Runbeck

No one is so rich that he or she can afford to lose a friend.

THE HERITAGE BOOK

T<small>OMORROW</small>, April 17, is the day that Benjamin Franklin, an American founding father and a past President of the United States, passed away.

Remembered as the first governor of Pennsylvania and later as President, he also gave us an array of practical and innovative devices and ideas used even to the present day.

It was Franklin, for example, who proposed Daylight Saving Time in 1786.

He enjoyed the warmth of a fire but not the smoke so he invented the Pennsylvania Fireplace, our Franklin Stove. This is an open, hooded, cast-iron hearth that captures and circulates warm air before allowing it to escape through the chimney. He also devised the "sliding plate" or damper.

Those of you who wear bifocal glasses have Benjamin Franklin to thank.

More than two hundred years after his death, Benjamin Franklin remains a fascinating figure who changed the world in small and large ways.

THE HERITAGE BOOK

Lord, behold our family here assembled.
We thank you for this place in which we dwell,
for the love that unites us,
for the peace accorded us this day,
for the hope with which we expect the morrow;
for the health, the work, the food and the bright
skies
that make our lives delightful;
for our friends in all parts of the earth.
Give us courage and gaiety and the quiet
mind.
Spare us to our friends, soften us to our
enemies.
Bless us, if it may be, in all our innocent
endeavours;
if it may not, give us the strength
to endure that which is to come
that we may be brave in peril,
constant in tribulation, temperate in wrath
and in all changes of fortune
and down to the gates of death,
loyal and loving to one another.
We beseech of you this help and mercy
For Christ's sake.

—Robert Louis Stevenson

MONDAY — APRIL 18

M ARG and I do volunteer work at our local school. Laurie, the teacher with whom I work, amused me today with these humorous signs of "burnout."

You know you have been teaching too long when:

You announce as you get off the bus "The left side was better behaved than the right side."

You tell your bridge partner to sit up straight.

The bank cashier points out that you have printed your signature.

You don't begin to speak at a party until everyone is quiet.

TUESDAY — APRIL 19

T HEY who teach their children to be thrifty and economical have already bequeathed them a fortune.

WEDNESDAY — APRIL 20

O NE of the heaviest burdens a person can carry is a chip on his or her shoulder.

THE HERITAGE BOOK

GIVE me a good digestion, Lord,
And also something to digest;
Give me a healthy body, Lord,
With sense to keep it at its best.

Give me a healthy mind, Lord,
To keep the good and pure in sight;
Which, seeing sin, is not appalled,
But finds a way to set it right.

Give me a sense of humour, Lord,
Give me the grace to see a joke;
To get some happiness from life,
And pass it on to other folk.

SOME people treat life like a slot machine, trying to put in as little as possible and hoping to hit the jackpot. Wiser people think of life as a solid investment from which they receive in terms of what they put in.

—Roger Hull

THE HERITAGE BOOK

SATURDAY — APRIL 23

THE following letter was sent by a Hamilton, Ontario gentleman to Eaton's Catalogue.

Dear Sirs,

I am told the T. Eaton Co. can furnish anything asked for. Now I lost my wife over a year ago and I am very lonely living alone. Can you send me a woman, not too old? I own my own house here. I have $67.00 a month income.

Perhaps this was the beginning of the computer date matching program.

SUNDAY — APRIL 24

"BEHOLD, an hour is coming and has already come, for you to be scattered, each to his own home, and to leave Me alone; and yet I am not alone, because the Father is with Me. These things I have spoken to you, that in Me you may have peace. In the world you have tribulation, but take courage; I have overcome the world."

—John 16: 32-33

MONDAY — APRIL 25

I LOVE the month of April! As the grass turns green and the crocus, hyacinth, and daffodil shoots peek through the soil it reminds me that the miracle of spring is never-ending.

In winter, as we look on the leafless branches and dreary landscape, it's hard to remember the beauty of spring and the opening of the budded leaves.

Suddenly, April returns and with it comes the flowers, the birds singing, and the sun, warmer and brighter.

April lifts my spirits and renews my hopes.

TUESDAY — APRIL 26

GETTING an idea should be like sitting down on a pin; it should make you jump up and do things.

WEDNESDAY — APRIL 27

NOSTALGIA is when you live life in the past lane.

FOR me the most difficult part of aging is the loss of old friends.

Barbara, a friend from childhood days to the present, passed away this morning at the Princess Margaret Hospital in Toronto.

To Barbara's family I offer Henry Ward Beecher's "Promise of God."

We have promises of God as thick as daisies in summer meadows, that death, which men most fear, shall be to us the most blessed of experiences, if we trust in Him. Death is unclasping; joy breaking out in the desert; the heart, come to blossoming time! Do we call it dying when the bud bursts into flower?

CHOOSE your life's mate carefully. From this one decision will come ninety percent of all your happiness or misery.

THE HERITAGE BOOK

My son-in-law Bruce is an avid golfer, so it was not surprising to see him leave early this morning, clubs in hand, for our nearby course. He and my grandson Marshall try to begin the season at the earliest possible moment.

On his return I asked what the best part of his game had been.

"It was Marshall's golf joke, Mother, and here it is:

'Why don't you play golf with Stan any more?' asked a wife one evening.

'Well,' replied her husband, 'would you play with a sneak who puts down the wrong score and moves his ball when you aren't looking?'

'I certainly would not!' said his wife.

'Well neither will Stan.'

"Mother, that joke is infinitely better than my game today!"

Enough said.

May

O Lord, from whom all good things do come. Grant to us thy humble servants, that by thy holy inspiration, we may think those things that be good, and by thy merciful guiding may perform the same; through our Lord Jesus Christ.

—The Book of Common Prayer

Love is the reason to greet the day, care about the future, and honour the past.

THE HERITAGE BOOK

MAY to me means roses,
Roses mean delight,
Graceful blooms unfolding
Petals red and white,
Luscious crimson clusters,
Buds of purest gold;
Who can measure roses
And the joy they hold.

May to me means roses,
Roses mean delight,
Fragrant blossoms shedding
Sweetness day and night;
Spicy damask odors—
Heavenly scents of tea,
God sends through his roses
Straight from Him to me.

Life should be like roses
In the month of May,
Bringing joy to others—
Making sad hearts gay;
Like the rose it withers—
Falls into decay;
Live then like the roses,
As you pass this way.

— Sarah Heinzerling

THE HERITAGE BOOK

MANY years ago my mother told us that garlic was very good for us. Later, I recall reading that garlic was good for the heart. Now it turns out that what I thought was just "an old wives' tale" passed from one generation to the next is, in fact, true.

Researchers have found that raw garlic juice, oil of garlic, and garlic supplements cause cholesterol levels to fall. In one experiment at an American university, volunteers consumed 1000 milligrams a day of deodorized garlic. Six months later they saw a drop of as much as 78 points in their blood cholesterol levels. Those who consumed no supplements had a three-point drop at best.

Not even the experts seem to know how the garlic works, but the evidence is undeniable.

It seems that no matter how much we rely on modern medicine to keep us healthy, there is still a secret store of medical folklore that has a basis in fact.

THE HERITAGE BOOK

<u>Thursday — May 5</u>

THE true gardeners of the world—those who look forward to quiet hours of nurturing and who treasure the beauty that springs from their care—know a calmness of spirit and a sense of accomplishment unlike any other.

—*Deana Deck*

<u>Friday — May 6</u>

LIVE so that when your children think of fairness, caring, and integrity, they think of you.

<u>Saturday — May 7</u>

THERE is a time to be born, and a time to die, says Solomon, and it is the memento of a truly wise man; but there is an interval between these two times of infinite importance.

—*C. A. Richmond*

Mother's Day

A MAN can build a mansion
Or a tiny cottage fair,
But it's not the hallowed place called "Home"
'Til Mother's dwelling there.

A man can build a mansion
With a high and spacious dome,
But no man in this world can build
That precious thing called "Home."

A man can build a mansion
Carting treasures o'er the foam,
Yes, a man can build the building
But a woman makes it "Home."

HAVE you ever noticed that when you ask how far it is to a certain place, country folk answer you in miles and city folk answer you in minutes?

THE HERITAGE BOOK

ALTHOUGH today's appliances are marvels of modern technology, there is one time-saver that I feel we could do without: the dishwasher.

Families of today don't know what they are missing. The time that we spent as a family washing and drying the dishes gave us time to talk about things that really mattered. When the girls were young we discussed school happenings, hair styles, or clothes. As they grew older, boyfriends became the main source of our conversations.

At family gatherings, cousins dried dishes and got to know one another better.

At one Christmas gathering the turkey platter was washed at least three times—I washed it, Julia dried it and then Mary, who was caught up in the discussion, put it back in the dirty dish pile.

Dishwashing is what people now call "quality time"—time spent together talking and sharing.

With a little luck maybe your dishwasher will break down.

Wednesday — May 11

Hail bounteous May, that dost inspire
Mirth and youth and warm desire!
Woods and groves are of thy dressing,
Hill and dale doth boast thy blessing.
                                    —*John Milton*

Thursday — May 12

Ascension Day

O Christ, Thou hast ascended
Triumphantly on high,
By cherub guards attended
And armies of the sky;
Let earth tell forth the story,—
Our very flesh and bone,
Emmanuel in glory.
Ascends His Father's throne.
                    —*The Book of Common Praise*

Friday — May 13

People who suffer from triskadiskaphobia—
this is your day to beware. Friday the 13th
is upon us!

THE HERITAGE BOOK

I GREW up in a small town on Canada's east coast. I enjoyed the comments of American actress Sissy Spacek, who was also a small-town girl.

"You know, I love cities, but it's nicer being able to go to the gas station in your home town and not even having to say 'Charge it.' You just say 'Hi Blue. Fill it up.' You can always depend on Blue. If it's snowing and you run off the road, Blue will come get you. Your word's your bond."

O NE thing have I desired of the Lord, that I will seek after; that I may dwell in the house of the Lord all the days of my life, to behold the beauty of the Lord, and to enquire in His Temple.

—Psalm 27: 4

W E are never more discontented with others than when we are discontented with ourselves.

THE HERITAGE BOOK

The Aging Letter Writer

JUST a line to say I'm living,
That I'm not among the dead,
Though I'm getting more forgetful,
And more mixed up in my head.

For, sometimes I can't remember
When I stand at the foot of stairs,
If I must go up for something,
Or I've just come down from there.

So, if it's my turn to write you
There's no need in getting sore.
I may think that I've written
And don't want to be a bore.

So, remember, I do love you
And I wish that you were here.
But now it's nearly mail time,
So, I must say "Goodbye, my dear."

There I stood beside the mailbox
With a face so very red
Instead of mailing you my letter
I had opened it instead.

THE HERITAGE BOOK

RECENTLY I found an old magazine in a long-forgotten trunk of memorabilia. It was *The Literary Digest* from the Funk and Wagnalls Company, dated July 1, 1916. It sold for the princely sum of 10 cents.

This issue contains stories of American intervention in Mexico, Democratic campaign issues, and a threatened rail strike. There was a section of "Current Poetry" and a criticism of playwright George Bernard Shaw's concept of Christianity.

What really caught my eye, however, were the advertisements. Eight full pages offered the "School and College Directory" for readers seeking "special educational advantages for their sons or daughters. A comprehensive selection of the best American Private Schools and Colleges is offered, each institution designed to meet various requirements."

Interestingly, two of the schools listed were Canadian. St. Andrews College offered "Careful Oversight, Thorough Instruction, Large Playing Fields and Excellent Situation."

Villa Maria, a convent girls' school in Montreal, offered "courtesy, refinement and discipline" along with "scholarship, sanitation and outdoor life."

THE HERITAGE BOOK

THURSDAY — MAY 19

IT is said that God gave us memory so we could have roses in winter. But it is also true that without memory we would not have a self in any season. The more memories you have, the more "you" you have.

—*George Will*

FRIDAY — MAY 20

A FRIEND's great-grandson, an 11-year-old, was asked to be the master of ceremonies at a community Boy Scouts' dinner.

"What I learned from speaking in front of a large audience," he told her afterwards, "is that everything on your body is soaking wet—except your throat."

SATURDAY — MAY 21

THE Japanese have a charming custom. Instead of honouring their great men with peerages or knighthoods, they give them the respectful title, "National Human Treasure."

—*Yousuf Karsh*

THE HERITAGE BOOK

Pentecost

O SING to the Lord a new song. For He has done wonderful things, His right hand and His holy arm have gained the victory for Him. The Lord has made known His salvation; He has revealed His righteousness in the sight of the nations. He has remembered His loving kindness and His faithfulness to the house of Israel; All the ends of the earth have seen the salvation of our God.

—*Psalm 98: 1-3*

MONDAY — MAY 23

A s has been our custom for many years, we are in Muskoka helping to open Eleanor's cottage, a "chore" we have come to love. This evening as we sat on the dock star-gazing I was reminded of the words of H. W. Longfellow:

Silently, one by one, in the infinite meadows of
    Heaven,
Blossomed the lovely stars, the forget-me-nots
    of the angels.

THE HERITAGE BOOK

TUESDAY — MAY 24

TODAY is the birthdate of Queen Victoria, the late British monarch. I have a feeling that had she been alive to see the sensationalistic coverage of all the exploits of the present-day "Royals" we might well have heard a repeat of her most famous quotation:

"We are not amused!"

WEDNESDAY — MAY 25

SOME critics are like chimney sweepers: they put out the fire below, or frighten the swallows from their nests above; they scrape a long time in the chimney, cover themselves with soot, and bring nothing away but a bag of cinders, and then sing from the top of the house as if they had built it.

—Longfellow

THURSDAY — MAY 26

WISDOM is knowing when you can't be wise.

—Paul Engle

THE HERITAGE BOOK

A POSTCARD with Mickey Mouse on the front came today from Emily, who was visiting Disney World, Florida. "Who was this man, Walt Disney?" I wondered and here is what I found out.

Walter Elias Disney was born December 5, 1901, in Chicago, Illinois, the fourth of five children. After working as an ambulance driver in World War One, he returned to the U.S. and worked for an advertising firm. At this time he made "Laugh-O-Grams," his first animated cartoons.

In 1923, Disney formed a partnership with his brother Roy, moved to Hollywood, and in 1925 married Lillian Marie Bounds. They had two daughters.

"Steamboat Willie," the first cartoon to use synchronized sound, appeared in 1928 and starred Mickey Mouse. "Snow White and the Seven Dwarfs," a full length film, was released in 1937.

In 1955, Disney opened Disneyland, a large theme amusement park. Five years after his death in 1966, Walt Disney World opened in Orlando, Florida.

He was a man who made children's dreams come alive.

Saturday — May 28

WHEN wealth is lost, nothing is lost; when health is lost, something is lost; when character is lost, all is lost.

—*German motto*

Sunday — May 29

TRUST in the Lord with all your heart, and do not lean on your own understanding. In all your ways acknowledge Him, and He will make your paths straight.

—*Proverbs 3: 5-6*

Monday — May 30

A RARE-BOOK collector met a man who said he had just thrown out an old Bible that had been packed away for generations.

"Somebody named Guten-something had printed it," said the man.

"Not Gutenburg!" gasped the collector, "You've thrown away one of the most famous books ever printed. It was priceless!"

"Oh well," the man replied, "Mine wouldn't have been worth much. Some man named Martin Luther scribbled notes all over it."

THE HERITAGE BOOK

I MARVEL at the advances in medical technology over the past few decades. Each new discovery, it seems, is even more miraculous than the one before.

I was reading recently about fetal surgery—surgery done on a baby while it is still a fetus in the mother's womb.

In 1983 Dr. Michael Harrison, a pioneer in fetal surgery, first tried to repair a lethal birth defect on a tiny fetus. The operation was a failure.

This first failure was followed by five more in as many years, but Dr. Harrison refused to give up.

Then in August, 1989, Blake Shultz was born, the first baby to have benefited from Dr. Harrison's revolutionary surgery to repair a defect known as diaphramatic hernia. Without the surgery he would surely have died.

From that time until now fetal surgery has improved and become almost routine.

It truly makes one wonder where technology will go in the 21st century.

June

GEORGE and I began our happy married life together on this date many years ago. Although I still miss him very much, I have some wonderful memories of our life together and particularly of our wedding day.

Someone once said, "Getting married is easy. Staying married is more difficult. Staying happily married for a lifetime should rank among the fine arts."

THE HERITAGE BOOK

JIM HENSON, puppeteer and creator of the Muppets, died in May of 1990. He was a creative genius and his death from pneumonia at age 53 came much too soon.

Thankfully, his "Sesame Street" tapes with his famous green felt frog, Kermit, muppets Bert and Ernie, Miss Piggy, and Big Bird are still being shown in North America as well as in many countries around the world.

One of the most poignant sympathy cards came from a Walt Disney Studios crew of designers—the Imagineers. It showed Mickey Mouse sitting on a log before a magnificent sunset, his arm draped around a downcast Kermit. A fitting tribute, I think.

MY garden, with its silence and the pulses of fragrance that come and go on the airy undulations, affects me like sweet music. Care stops at the gates and gazes at me wistfully through the bars. Among my flowers and trees, Nature takes me into her own hands and I breathe freely as the first man.

—Alexander Smith

SATURDAY — JUNE 4

A FRIEND was trying to encourage his elderly mother to enjoy the money she had accumulated through years of frugal living. "Mother, you have enough money to last you until you're a hundred."

"And then what will I do?"

SUNDAY — JUNE 5

BE strong and of good courage, fear not, nor be afraid . . . for the Lord thy God, He it is that doth go with thee; He will not fail thee, nor forsake thee.

—Deuteronomy 31: 6

MONDAY — JUNE 6

I KNOW the world is filled with trouble and many injustices. But reality is as beautiful as it is ugly. I think it is just as important to sing about beautiful mornings as it is to talk about slums. I just couldn't write anything without hope in it.

—Oscar Hammerstein II

Tuesday — June 7

Marg and I took advantage of today's beautiful weather by walking down to the millpond. We had brought books with us and it was so pleasant to sit on the benches by the water to read.

Marg also brought a special treat in her thermos for us to share. It is called a fruit juice spritzer. For those of you looking for a refreshing but light summer drink, here is the recipe.

2 cups low-calorie cranberry-raspberry
    drink (chilled)
12 ounces club soda (chilled)
2 slices of orange with peel
mint sprigs (optional)

Cut each orange slice in half. Put 1 piece in each of 4 tall glasses. Pour 1/2 cup cranberry-raspberry drink into each glass. Fill with club soda. Garnish with sprigs of mint. Serves 4— calories per serving: 27.

On very hot summer days, ice cubes are a welcome addition to keep the drink really chilled. Marg suggests freezer-frosting the glasses for extra special occasions.

THE HERITAGE BOOK

GOOD intentions, like choice fruit, are perishable and difficult to keep.

As you know, I do volunteer work at our local school. Imagine my shock today as I walked into the room and twenty-two young voices shouted "Surprise!"

It seems their teacher knew that today was my birthday and had suggested it would be nice to make a "Happy Birthday" card for me. The children's enthusiasm bubbled over. "Not just a card, a party" they insisted and so when I walked into the room I was moved to near-tears. These little darlings had hung streamers, made tissue flowers, and cut, coloured, or painted on an enormous poster-size card which read "Happy Birthday to our best story reader!" It was signed by every child.

The "pièce de résistance" was a beautiful cake, obviously baked and decorated by the children and covered in candles.

I don't think I have ever enjoyed a birthday party more.

THE HERITAGE BOOK

<u>F<small>RIDAY</small> — J<small>UNE</small> 10</u>

My friend Wilma included this lovely poem in her letter to me today. It is by Lois Sears and is titled "Ambition."

I would not ask for wealth nor fame,
For temporal things of earth,
But that all men might speak my name
In terms of honoured worth.

"His word's his bond. He would not lie,
Nor idle words repeat.
His life is ruled by ideals high
His soul knows no defeat."

No pompous words, no vain display
No deed that bards may pen
But having passed, may friends but say:
"He loved his fellow men."

<u>S<small>ATURDAY</small> — J<small>UNE</small> 11</u>

P<small>RESERVE</small>, within a wild sanctuary,
An inaccessible valley of reveries.
                                        —*Ellen Glasgow*

THE HERITAGE BOOK

<u>SUNDAY — JUNE 12</u>

THEY that trust in the Lord shall be as Mount Zion, which cannot be removed, but abideth forever. As the mountains are round about Jerusalem, so is the Lord around His people from henceforth even for ever.

—Psalm 125: 1-2

<u>MONDAY — JUNE 13</u>

IF you see ten troubles coming down the road, you can be sure that nine will run into the ditch before they reach you.

—Calvin Coolidge

<u>TUESDAY — JUNE 14</u>

JAKE FRAMPTON stopped by this evening as Bruce was mowing the lawn.

"I had planned to cut my lawn this weekend, but my neighbour borrowed my mower," said Jake. "As a matter of fact he borrowed every mower on our street," laughed Jake, "because he said that this was one weekend that he intended to sleep in—in peace."

THE HERITAGE BOOK

FRIENDS of mine recently celebrated their fiftieth wedding anniversary in a delightful way. Their family sent them on an Alaskan cruise and this evening a group of friends and family got together to enjoy their films, photos and stories of this fabulous trip.

They boarded their ship in Vancouver. The cruise follows the "Inside Passage" up the British Columbia coastline to Ketchikan, Alaska. The scenery on this route is spectacular: glacier-clad mountains, porpoises swimming in the deep channels, waterfalls tumbling down the cliffs, miles and miles of pine-treed wilderness.

Ketchikan, Alaska's first city, is built on stilts—the main street is actually a boardwalk—and boasts more totem poles than anywhere else in the world.

On to Juneau and then Glacier Bay National Park, where the photos showed crystal cliffs of exquisite beauty.

Sitka, a town with a rehabilitation centre for eagles, is the last stop before the cruise back to Vancouver.

It was truly a spectacular way to celebrate fifty years of happiness.

THURSDAY — JUNE 16

ONCE I knew the depth where no hope was and darkness lay on the face of all things. Then love came and set my soul free. Once I fretted and beat myself against the wall that shut me in. My life was without a past or future, and death was a consummation devoutly to be wished. But a little word from the fingers of another fell into my hands and clutched at emptiness, and my heart leaped up with the rapture of living. I do not know the meaning of the darkness, but I have learned the overcoming of it.

—Helen Keller

FRIDAY — JUNE 17

WHAT riches are ours in the world of nature, from the majesty of a distant peak to the fragile beauty of a tiny flower, and all without cost to us, the beholders! No man is poor who has watched a sunrise or who keeps a mountain in his heart.

—Esther Baldwin York

THE HERITAGE BOOK

FAILURES are divided into two classes—those who thought and never did, and those who did and never thought.

O worship the King
All glorious above;
O gratefully sing
His power and His love;
Our shield and Defender,
The Ancient of days,
Pavilioned in splendour,
And girded with praise.

THERE are two ways to sufficiency and happiness. We may either diminish our wants or augment our means; either will do—the result is the same. But if you are wise, you will do both at the same time; and if you are very wise, you will do both in such a way as to augment the general happiness of society.

—Benjamin Franklin

THE HERITAGE BOOK

HERE are some of my favourite verses from the poem "June" by B. H. Warr.

Now comes June, all garlanded with roses,
Lightly stepping o'er the dew-kissed mead,
Robed in tender green and shod with silver
Slim and slender as a windswept reed.

Rosy as the dawn with eyes like starshine
Spun gold in a halo round her head;
Like a winsome bride, she walks in beauty;
Flowers blossom where her white feet tread.

Golden days she brings, and twilight
    evenings,
Purple shadows dark across the lawn;
Lustrous nights, silvered by moonlight magic,
And opal skies aglow at early dawn.

June, beloved of poets and of lovers,
Blending heaven and earth in perfect tune
Bringing beauty of both Spring and Summer
Loveliest month of all the year—sweet June.

<u>Wednesday — June 22</u>

To learn from our successes is wise; to learn from our failures is vital.

—William Arthur Ward

<u>Thursday — June 23</u>

I have always been a "morning person" but many of my family and friends are not so. My grandson-in-law Bill, who is a doctor, recently copied an article in one of his medical journals that offered advice on having more energy in the morning.

Have a good wholesome dinner in the evening but don't eat or snack right before you go to sleep. It turns on the digestive system and can keep you awake.

Sleep between six to eight hours. Too little or too much sleep will leave you tired in the morning.

To ensure a deep, restful sleep, don't go to bed until you are about to nod off. As soon as you wake up fully, get out of bed.

Once you are up, exercise for a few minutes and then shower.

Have a glass of fruit juice (a good energizer), and eat a high-fibre cereal and a piece of fruit.

FRIDAY — JUNE 24

HAPPY laughter and family voices in the home will keep more kids off the streets at night than the loudest curfew.

SATURDAY — JUNE 25

IF you outlive a worthy opponent, you will find that you miss him.

—Bismarck

SUNDAY — JUNE 26

BE strong and of good courage; be not afraid, neither be thou dismayed: for the Lord thy God is with thee whithersoever thou goest.

—Joshua 1: 9

MONDAY — JUNE 27

JUDGE your success by the degree that you're enjoying peace, health and love.

—H. Jackson Brown Jr.

THE HERITAGE BOOK

TUESDAY — JUNE 28

WHETHER seventy or sixteen, there is in every being's heart the love of wonder, the sweet amazement at the stars and the starlike things and thoughts, the undaunted challenge of events, the unfailing childlike appetite for what next, and the joy and the game of life.

You are as young as your faith, as old as your doubt; as young as your self-confidence, as old as your fear; as young as your hope, as old as your despair.

WEDNESDAY — JUNE 29

A POLITICIAN thinks of the next election; a statesman, of the next generation.

—James Freeman Clarke

THURSDAY — JUNE 30

OF the few innocent pleasures left to men past middle life, the jamming of common sense down the throats of fools is perhaps the keenest.

—T.H. Huxley

July

Canada Day

O GOD our Heavenly Father
We lift our hearts to Thee.
In thankfulness and gladness
We sing from sea to sea;
For thou hast richly blessed us
With countless gifts of love,
And always Thou hast showered us
With mercies from above.
— *Reverend Kenneth Moyer*

THE HERITAGE BOOK

M<small>ARY</small> McConnell and her large family left for the cottage today. I asked Mary what she felt was the most important item to remember and she answered without hesitation, "The first-aid kit. We can forget pillows, towels, and even children but not the first-aid kit."

Mary suggests a container that is waterproof (and mouse-proof) and well marked with a large red cross and the words FIRST AID. In her kit she includes: clear, concise first-aid manual, six 1 inch roller bandages, 6 2-inch roller bandages, 6 large gauze pressure bandages, 12 3x3-inch sterile gauze dressings, 12 4x4-inch sterile gauze dressings, 2 sterile surgical pads, 1 large non-stick burn dressing, 2 rolls 1-inch waterproof adhesive tape, 36 adhesive strips, 6 triangular bandages, 1 box of cotton-tipped swabs, antiseptic soap, rubbing alcohol, 1 pair heavy duty first-aid scissors, 6 large safety pins, tweezers, sharp sewing needle, thermometer, ice pack, sunburn ointment, notepad and pencil, and last, but very important, phone numbers of the local ambulance, police and fire departments.

They will be well prepared for any emergency.

Sunday — July 3

But let those who take refuge in Thee be glad, let them ever sing for joy; and mayest Thou shelter them, that those who love Thy name may exult in Thee. For it is Thou who dost bless the righteous man, O Lord, that dost surround him with favour as with a shield.

—*Psalm 5: 11-12*

Monday — July 4

This is Independence Day south of the border, a day when Americans, young and old, celebrate with an exuberant show of patriotism.

William Tyler Page wrote "The American Creed" and I believe these last few lines of this piece are a fitting tribute to this great nation.

"I therefore believe it is my duty to my country to love it; to support its Constitution; to obey its laws; to respect its flag; and to defend it against all enemies."

THE HERITAGE BOOK

TUESDAY — JULY 5

UNLESS a man hammers morality home to his heirs, he has not built for them a strong foundation upon which to build their lives.

—*Cameron Caine*

WEDNESDAY — JULY 6

MURIEL tells me that her husband Will has started his day in the same way for as long as she can remember.

"He gets out of bed, walks over to the open window and spends a few minutes surveying all that is before him. Then he takes a few deep breaths of the morning air and says 'Well, God's done his part; now it's my turn.'"

THURSDAY — JULY 7

LIVE every day as if it were your last. Do every job as if you were the boss. Drive as if all other vehicles were police cars. Treat everybody else as if they were you.

THE HERITAGE BOOK

ON the brow of a hill overlooking Toronto the striking silhouette of a massive castle dominates the skyline and stirs the imagination. This magnificent structure was built using the most pleasing elements of Norman, Gothic and Romanesque styles of architecture. Incredibly, it was built as a home for Sir Henry Mill Pellatt, a prominent Canadian financier, industrialist and military officer of the early 20th century, and his wife Lady Pellatt.

Today, Casa Loma is an important tourist attraction in a city that boasts such sights as the C.N. Tower and the SkyDome. The elegance and opulence of its rooms are extraordinary.

The Conservatory features a stained glass dome; the Pellatt family crest can be found in the library ceiling; and the Oak Room has intricately carved panelling that is breathtaking.

Our seniors' bus tour today gave us hours to explore the castle and its gardens with their unique fountains and sculptures.

Casa Loma is open year round and it is a visit that people of all ages will enjoy.

THE HERITAGE BOOK

GENIUS is an infinite capacity for taking pains.

—Jane Ellice Hopkins

REST of the weary,
Joy of the sad,
Hope of the dreary,
Light of the glad,
Home of the stranger,
Strength to the end,
Refuge from danger,
Saviour and friend.

—Reverend J.S.B. Monsell

HOW strange is the use of our language: "hill" and "hump" are largely synonymous, yet we speak of "over the hump" meaning progression and "over the hill" meaning regression.

—A. Sheppard Jr.

THE HERITAGE BOOK

<u>TUESDAY — JULY 12</u>

IMMORTALITY lies not in the things you leave behind, but in the people that your life has
touched.

<u>WEDNESDAY — JULY 13</u>

WHO hath a book
Has friends at hand,
And gold and gear
At his command;

And rich estates,
If he but look,
Are held by him
Who hath a book.

Who hath a book
Has but to read
And he may be
A king indeed;

His kingdom is
His inglenook;
All that is his
Who hath a book.

—William Nesbit

THE HERITAGE BOOK

THE number of Canadians 65 years and older is growing dramatically. By the year 2020 it is predicted that nearly one in every five Canadians will be over 65. There are many reasons for this startling statistic, but one of the most important is that people over 55 are in better health than they used to be.

Leading an active, healthy lifestyle requires a nutritious and balanced diet. Since older people generally require less food than younger adults, it is even more important that what they do eat is healthful.

Keeping active mentally, physically, and socially also plays a large role in good health. Volunteer work and membership in clubs and organizations are but a few of the ways that we seniors may choose to occupy our time. Many universities offer free tuition to people over 65, giving us a chance to learn things that we always wanted to know but for which we never had the time.

As well, many older adults are looking into alternative housing options, including communities that eliminate daily chores such as laundry, shopping, shovelling snow, gardening, etc.

May your own senior years be happy, fulfilling ones.

Friday — July 15

Today in the late afternoon Justin and Jenny and I went for a lovely walk in the woods behind the millpond. The afternoon light shone down between the leaves and the shadows danced on the path in front of us. We sat on a large log for several minutes and listened to the summer sounds around us—the hum of a mosquito, the chattering of two squirrels, and the high-pitched hum of the tree frogs.

These lines by Longfellow came to mind:

"Pleasant it was, when woods were green, and winds were soft and low,

To lie amid some sylvan scene,

Where, the long drooping boughs between, shadows dark and sunlight sheen alternate come and go."

Saturday — July 16

An idealist is one who, on noticing that a rose smells better than a cabbage, concludes that it will also make better soup.

—H.L. Mencken

THE HERITAGE BOOK

SUNDAY — JULY 17

THE commonest and cheapest of all pleasures is conversation. It is the greatest pastime of life.

—Bryne Hope Sanders

MONDAY — JULY 18

THE old axe looked at the load of time
  stacked up at the edge of the year:
there were four long seasons, twelve long
    months,
and fifty-two weeks lying near.
The axe's job was to split them up
into days and hours and minutes,
his one concern that he not grow dull,
unaware of the paradox in it.

For the sharpest minds and keenest edge
accrue to the busiest folks
who are kindling fires, warming friends,
instead of counting strokes.
And counter to claim, the year never ends—
there is always more wood to hew—
yet those with the fewest axes to grind
are those with the most to do.

—Alma Barkman

TUESDAY — JULY 19

A GEM is not polished without rubbing, nor a man perfected without trials.

—*Chinese proverb*

WEDNESDAY — JULY 20

THOSE of you who enjoy baseball but feel that players are overpaid will enjoy Pete Incaviglia's explanation of why ball players are not overpaid.

Said the Texas Rangers' outfielder a few years ago, "People think we make three million or four million dollars a year. They don't realize that most of us make only $500 000."

THURSDAY — JULY 21

THE reward of great men is that, long after they have died, one is not quite sure that they are dead.

—*Jules Renard*

THE HERITAGE BOOK

A TEAM is where a boy can prove his courage, on his own, on what he can do himself, or what he can contribute to the team's good. A gang is where a coward goes to hide.

—Mickey Mantle

SATURDAY — JULY 23

TODAY is a very special anniversary for Marg and Bruce. Thirty years ago today they exchanged wedding vows, and this evening we enjoyed a delightful reunion with several members of their wedding party.

Unknown to Marg and Bruce, Marshall and Phyllis were able to get in touch with the maid of honour, the best man, and one of the ushers. These three, along with their spouses, arrived together to give us all a fun evening of home movies, photographs, and hilarious stories of the joyous occasion.

This was the first time in many years that this group of friends had been together, and it was the wee hours of the morning before the conversation slowed down.

Good times are always better when shared with old friends.

THE HERITAGE BOOK

BEHOLD, I stand at the door and knock; if anyone hears My voice and opens the door, I will come in to him, and will dine with him, and he with Me.

—Revelation 3: 20

I ENJOYED Jim Fiebig's comments on welcome tricks of the mind:

"Because we live 3000 kilometres apart, I see my parents maybe once every couple of years. I always dread the first few seconds of each reunion, when I am sadly aware that they look older than they looked before.

"I don't want my parents to get old. And that must be why, after those first few seconds of the reunion, the years somehow vanish from their faces. They become young before my eyes, and I am able to say with all conscious sincerity, 'Gee, you guys haven't aged a bit.'"

TUESDAY — JULY 26

I MUST confess that there are a few "advancements" in technology that I really don't care for. For example, when I use the telephone I really dislike "talking to" a computer.

When we call information for a number this strange computer voice says "The number is. . . . I repeat, the number is. . . . If your pencil breaks as you're writing the number you can't say, "Just a second, I need a new pencil."

When we first owned a telephone all of our calls went through the operator.

"Ida, could you put me through to Isabelle Smith please."

"Why sure Edna. How are the girls today? Please tell George how much I enjoyed Sunday's sermon. I'm ringing Isabelle right now."

I really miss Ida. I really miss real operators with real voices who ask me real questions. I dislike talking with a computer and I really dislike being corrected by a machine, "Please answer the question with just 'yes' or 'no'!" I can't even use "please."

WEDNESDAY — JULY 27

THERE is something that is much more scarce, something finer by far, than ability. It is the ability to recognize ability.

—*Elbert Hubbard*

THURSDAY — JULY 28

"THERE are toothbrushes that have a miniature music box in the handle that play the song of your choice—if you brush correctly. Tunes run for ninety seconds, the time the inventor says is required for a good brushing."

I saw this story in a ten-year-old dental magazine and I thought that it sounded like a super invention. I have a feeling however that I may be just a little late with my order.

FRIDAY — JULY 29

THE best safety device in a car is a rear view mirror with a police officer in it.

THE HERITAGE BOOK

<u>Saturday — July 30</u>

I RECEIVED a letter today from my good friend Maria Sanchez, who lives in California.

Maria's granddaughter Natalia has Down Syndrome. Maria was excited to tell me about a program called "Project Child" of which Natalia is a member.

"Every six weeks Natalia goes off to spend a weekend with the Richter family, John, Louise, and their daughters, Julia and Josie. The National Down Syndrome Society, through Project Child, brought Natalia and this family together.

"It encourages independance in Natalia, gives her parents a planned weekend break, and offers the host families a chance to open their homes and hearts to a special child.

"Many people who haven't spent time with these kids fear them. This gives others a chance to understand and learn tolerance of those who are different."

I think it's a wonderful idea.

<u>Sunday — July 31</u>

B ETTER are the poor who walk in their integrity than they who are crooked though they be rich.

August

Hail August: Maiden of the sultry days,
To thee I bring the measured need of
praise
For, though thou hast besmirched the day
and night,
And hid a wealth of glory from our sight,
Thou still dost build in musing pensive mood,
Thy blissful idylls in the underwood.
Thou still dost yield new beauties, fair and
young,
With many a form of grace as yet unsung,
Which ripens o'er thy pathway and repays
The toil and langour of the sultry days.

—*Charles Mair*

THE HERITAGE BOOK

Is there anything more enjoyable than a summer picnic? Yesterday's holiday gave us the perfect chance to enjoy a visit to the city and a basket lunch. We spent the day on Toronto's Centre Island, a place I hadn't been to in many years.

We parked downtown and joined the throngs of people in line to board the ferry. The beautiful weather seemed to have encouraged half the population of Toronto to enjoy the cooling lake breezes on the island.

Once on the island, we walked the trails, watched as young children enjoyed the rides and the animal petting zoo, and then we found a perfect picnic area. It was a shaded place with a lovely view of the lake.

It was dusk when we caught the ferry returning to the city, and the stars were just beginning to twinkle in the sky over the harbour.

Sometimes we forget that we have many beautiful places to visit within an easy driving distance of home. Toronto's Centre Island is certainly one of those places.

THE HERITAGE BOOK

TIME flies, but remember, you're the navigator.

IN this hot weather, backyard pools get a lot of use. Fortunately the laws in our area require pool owners to maintain good fences to keep out adventuresome children.

Our neighbours have a lovely in-ground pool and three small children. They have wisely chosen to have their children wear life jackets from the time they get up until the time they go to bed. As they told me, "Toddlers have drowned even when several adults have been present, but have not been paying attention." Their children have been taught to swim but the life jackets provide extra protection—and peace of mind for their parents.

LOVE doesn't make the world go round. Love is what makes the ride worthwhile.

—*F.P. Jones*

Eventide

GOD loves the Aged.
He gives them greater visions than the
    young;
He puts the word of wisdom on their tongue;
And keeps His presence ever by their side,
From dawn to dusk, and on through eventide.

God helps the Aged.
Within their home His Spirit ever dwells;
Their mellow hearts are touched like chiming
    bells;
He calms their fears, then worries disappear,
Because they know His help is always near.

God keeps the Aged.
With hearts of gold, and silver-tinted hair,
And earnestness, and greater faith in prayer;
He keeps them as a shepherd guards his
    sheep,
'Til in his fold they gently fall asleep.
                 —Charles T.H. Bancroft

THE HERITAGE BOOK

IT is not easy to be still in this rough and rest-
less world. Yet God says "Be still"; and He
says also, "In returning and rest shall ye be
saved; in quietness and confidence shall be
your strength."

—Isaiah 30: 15

I ARRIVED in Muskoka yesterday for my annual
visit with Eleanor. The clean fresh air already has me in its grip—I slept in until nearly
nine this morning. (I am *sure* that staying up
talking until two o'clock in the morning had
nothing to do with my tardy rising.)

Muskoka is one of my favourite places, and I
feel so lucky to be able to visit this beautiful
area in the company of such an old and trea-
sured friend.

The coal-burning steamship R.M.S. Segwun
sounded her horn as she passed by this morning. Although I was just waking, I hurried out
to the porch to watch her sail by. The Segwin
is a part of our Canadian heritage and I feel
proud each time I see her.

THE HERITAGE BOOK

TUESDAY — AUGUST 9

JOSEPH PULITZER's advice to writers could apply to anyone who is communicating with others:

"Put it before them briefly so they will read it, clearly so they will appreciate it, picturesquely so they will remember it and, above all, accurately so they will be guided by its light."

WEDNESDAY — AUGUST 10

I OWE much to my friends. But, all things considered, it strikes me that I owe even more to my enemies. The real person springs to life under a sting, even better than under a caress.

—*André Gide*

THE HERITAGE BOOK

Watching a sculler row by in the early morning mist, I was reminded of an incredible tale of courage from the 1992 Olympics.

Silken Laumann, 1991 world champion sculler, seemed to be a "best bet" for a gold medal at Barcelona until a freak accident on May 16. A German men's pairs boat rammed Laumann's craft, the bow smashing into her lower right leg, slicing her skin and causing severe muscle, ligament, nerve and bone damage. Her Olympic dream appeared to have ended. She endured four operations, significant weight loss, and tremendous pain but she was determined: she would compete in the XXVth Olympiad.

In her hospital bed she lifted weights. By mid-June she could walk with crutches, but she was back on the water, her boat modified to allow her to row with her injured leg in a special brace.

Despite the odds against her, Silken Laumann made the finals. With all of Canada cheering, she rowed a magnificent final race, earning the Bronze Medal.

As she explained, "My goal in sport has always, always been to be the best that I can be."

FRIDAY — AUGUST 12

IT was a glorious Muskoka day! Sunshine, blue skies, and sparkling water welcomed us on the lake today.

Eleanor and I enjoyed a voyage up Lake Muskoka to the Indian River and into the town of Port Carling. This pretty town is where the Muskoka Lakes come together.

Today we shopped at the grocery store right by the docks, and wandered through the pretty shops at "Steamboat Bay" right on the shore of Lake Muskoka.

We lunched on the deck of the local hotel before heading back down the river on our return cruise to the cottage.

Memories are made of days like today.

SATURDAY — AUGUST 13

THE God of Music dwelleth out of doors.

—*Edith Matilda Thomas*

SUNDAY — AUGUST 14

IWILL love thee, O Lord, my strength; the Lord is my stony rock, and my defense; my Saviour, my God, and my might, in whom I will trust, my buckler, the horn also of my salvation, and my refuge.

—Psalm 18: 1

MONDAY — AUGUST 15

LAST night we watched in awe a display of the Northern Lights.

Although I have often seen streaks of light in the northern sky during August, it is frequently difficult to tell if they are in fact the "aurora borealis." But there could be no mistake last evening. As we watched, large jagged streaks lit up the sky and "danced" back and forth, up and down, and side to side.

The show lasted for almost two hours. We sat in our comfortable wooden chairs and marvelled at nature's incredible display. It was a sight I will never forget.

THE HERITAGE BOOK

TUESDAY — AUGUST 16

WE have no more right to consume happiness without producing it than to consume wealth without producing it.

—George Bernard Shaw

WEDNESDAY — AUGUST 17

DON'T judge with haste your fellow men.
See only what is fine and true.
Ignore the worst—bring out the best—
And take the charitable view.
I hope God does the same for us—
And sees the virtues, not the vice . . .
If He remembered only faults—
Who'd ever get to Paradise?

—Patience Strong

THURSDAY — AUGUST 18

LARGE minds discuss ideas. Average minds discuss events. Small minds discuss people.

THE HERITAGE BOOK

ELEANOR and I spent a lovely day at one of the resorts here in Muskoka. Friends of ours are enjoying a vacation at Aston Resort, near Bracebridge on Lake Muskoka, and it was a pleasure to visit with them at this outstanding hotel.

Aston is built on the rocks high above the lake. The view from the rooms is marvellous— you can see for miles across the lake.

For water sports enthusiasts, there is swimming, sunning, surfing, sailing, and waterskiing. A delightful group of young people work down by the water and their enthusiasm is an encouragement to try any and all of the equipment.

For families with young children there is a child-care program that gives parents a holiday while allowing the children to participate in many and varied activities.

We enjoyed lunch on the wooden terrace overlooking the lake. There was a barbecue with a salad bar, along with many other tempting dishes.

Aston Resort is a vacation spot with something for all ages. I hope to return in the fall for one of their special "Senior Tours."

THE HERITAGE BOOK

SATURDAY — AUGUST 20

A WALK in the woods today gave us hints that autumn is not far off. The squirrels seemed to be working more quickly, secreting the nuts for winter; scarlet and yellow leaves are showing on many trees and there is a slight chill in the early morning and late evening air.

Blue to the north is a sky so clear
It means the corner of the year
Has been turned, from now on all
Leaves and men face to the Fall.
—Robert P. Tristan Coffin

SUNDAY — AUGUST 21

L ET him who means to love life and see good days, refrain his tongue from evil and his lips from speaking guile. And let him turn away from evil and do good; let him seek peace and pursue it.

—1 Peter 3: 10-11

MONDAY — AUGUST 22

F ORGIVENESS is the fragrance the violet sheds on the heel that crushed it.

THE HERITAGE BOOK

Out of this Life

Out of this life I shall never take
Things of silver and gold I make;
All that I cherish and hoard away
After I leave, on earth must stay.

Though I have toiled for a painting rare
To hang on my wall I must leave it there.
Though I call it mine and boast its worth
I must give it up when I quit this earth.

All that I gather and all that I keep,
I must leave behind when I fall asleep.

And I wonder, often, just what shall I own
In that other life when I pass alone.
What shall He find and what shall He see
In the soul that answers the call for me?

Shall the great Judge learn, when my task is
    through,
That my soul had gathered some riches
    too?
Or shall at the last it be mine to find,
    That all I had worked for I had left behind?
                                    —*Author unknown*

WEDNESDAY — AUGUST 24

A WALK through our neighbourhood today gave Lila MacGuinness and me a chance to survey all of the gardens whose growth is really at a peak right now.

The gardens I appreciated most were those where wildflowers grew in abundance. Lila told me there are tins for sale now that are filled with a wide variety of wildflower seed.

Planted in spring, they will cover a large area of your garden. They are easily tended, hardy blooms which grow and multiply each year. They would seem to be perfect for "non-gardeners" who enjoy the look but not the hard work of a beautiful garden.

THURSDAY — AUGUST 25

F ORGET thyself; console the sadness near thee:
Thine own shall then depart,
And songs of joy, like heavenly birds, shall cheer thee
And dwell within thy heart.

THE HERITAGE BOOK

THE best remedy for those who are afraid, lonely or unhappy is to go outside, somewhere where they can be quite alone with the heavens, nature, and God. Because only then does one feel that all is as it should be and that God wishes to see people happy, amidst the simple beauty of nature. As long as this exists, and it certainly always will, I know that then there will always be comfort for every sorrow, whatever the circumstances may be.

—The Diary of Ann Frank

MY son-in-law John missed last week's adult discussion group so he tried to review this evening by asking "What did you talk about last week?" He laughed as the group answered as one, "You!"

BUT these have been written that you may believe that Jesus is the Christ, the Son of God; and that believing you may have life in His name.

—John 20: 31

THE HERITAGE BOOK

<u>MONDAY — AUGUST 29</u>

THE joyful noise of children's voices is sounding in our neighbourhood again.

John, a 14-year old, stopped by this evening, pleased as punch with all of his new camp jokes. I present to you my favourite.

An elderly cat went to an "old cat's home" and saw the group sitting in rocking chairs purring. "That's not for me," he said and he travelled on. Soon he came upon a group of cats dancing on a fence, "That's not for me either," he said sadly. Then he saw a lot of mice on skateboards. "Now that's for me! Meals on wheels!"

<u>TUESDAY — AUGUST 30</u>

A LOVING heart is the truest wisdom.

—*Charles Dickens*

<u>WEDNESDAY — AUGUST 31</u>

FOR good or ill, your conversation is your advertisement. Every time you open your mouth, you let men look into your mind.

—*Bruce Barton*

September

September

A SOLEMN hush broods o'er the peaceful land,
The birds flit, voiceless in the changing
  trees
The sumach lights its torch on every hand,
The golden rod nods in the quiet breeze,
A hint of frost, when sinks the sun to rest;
A mist of white when breaks the dawn of day;
And in the whisper of the mild southwest
We catch the word that Summer's passed
  away.

—*H.B. Anderson*

FRIDAY — SEPTEMBER 2

To improve the golden moment of opportunity and catch the good that is within our reach, is the great art of life.

—Samuel Johnson

SATURDAY — SEPTEMBER 3

SEE if this sounds familiar to you: "We at present live in an essentially fast age. . . . The rush and excitement that our everyday life calls for did not exist three quarters of a century ago, and consequently the tax upon the mind, and the wear and tear on the homelife of the present generation is, as a whole, full of ceaseless activity. The sensational events that the newspapers recount reach the various homes, and are too often discussed before children and cannot but have a stimulating effect on their brains. . . . In other words, the life of today is productive of nerve excitability, followed by exhaustion."

It is interesting to note that the above was written by Frances H. Rankin, M.D. in 1890. Apparently every generation complains—about the same things.

THE HERITAGE BOOK

Hɪs delight is in the law of the Lord. And he shall be like a tree planted by the rivers of water, that bringeth forth his fruits in his season; his leaf also shall not wither; and whatsoever he doeth shall prosper.

—Psalm 1: 2, 3

Labour Day

Iғ you work for a man, in heaven's name work for him. If he pays wages that supply you your bread and butter, work for him, speak well of him, think well of him and stand by the institution he represents. . . .

I pray you, so long as you are a part of an institution, do not condemn it. Not that you will injure the institution—not that—but when you disparage the concern of which you are a part, you disparage yourself.

—Elbert Hubbard

THE HERITAGE BOOK

IT's back to school today for the children in our area. My granddaughter Phyllis passes along this "Teacher's Prayer" for today.

I want to teach my students how
To live this life on earth,
To face its struggles and its strife
And to improve their worth.
Not just the lesson in a book,
Or how the rivers flow,
But to choose the proper path
Wherever they may go.
To understand eternal truth
And know the right from wrong,
And gather all the beauty of
A flower and a song.
For if I help the world to grow
In wisdom and in grace,
Then I shall feel that I have won
And I have filled my place.
And so I ask your guidance, God,
That I may do my part,
For character and confidence
And happiness of heart.

THE HERITAGE BOOK

MARG and I had a good laugh today as we listened to our young neighbours Nathaniel and Natasha discuss their first days of classes.

"It was just wonderful, Mrs. McCann," Natasha enthused. "We had spelling and art and I just loved fitness. I have new pencil crayons and my locker partner is great." She bubbled on and on with great enthusiasm about her whole experience.

Nathaniel had quite a different reaction. "It was awful. We had spelling and art and I can't draw. In fitness we had to do some dumb exercises, I lost my new pencil case, and my locker partner is a *girl*."

I am sure Nathaniel will adjust.

MEN grow when inspired by a high purpose when contemplating vast horizons. The sacrifice of oneself is not very difficult for one burning with the passion for a great adventure.
—*Alexis Carrel*

Friday — September 9

Visits always give us pleasure—if not the arrival, the departure.

—Portugese proverb

Saturday — September 10

Nothing is ever lost by courtesy. It is the cheapest of the pleasures; costs nothing and conveys much. It pleases him who gives and him who receives, and thus, like mercy, is twice blessed.

—Erastus Wiman

Sunday — September 11

The land has produced its harvest; God, our God, has blessed us. God has blessed us; may people everywhere honour him.

—Psalm 67: 6-7

Monday — September 12

There are two kinds of helpers: those who give advice and those who peel potatoes.

THE HERITAGE BOOK

ONE thing that surprises college graduates most when they get out in the world is finding out just how much uneducated people know.

Go confidently in the direction of your dreams! Live the life you've imagined! As you simplify your life, the laws of the universe will be simpler, solitude will not be solitude, poverty will not be poverty, nor weakness weakness.

—*Henry David Thoreau*

THE sun with all those planets moving around it can ripen the smallest bunch of grapes as if it had nothing else to do. Why then should I doubt His power?

—*Galileo*

THE HERITAGE BOOK

A thousand words will not leave so deep an impression as one deed.

—Henrik Ibsen

At this time of year our family gets a great deal of pleasure from the "Fall Fair."

There is always something for each of us: the younger children head straight to the animal barns, many of the adults enjoy the displays of farm produce, and I like to see the arts and crafts presentations.

This year Justin and Jenny entered their dog in the "most unusual-looking dog" category, where he was a respectable runner-up. "Mutt" was narrowly edged out by a dog closely resembling a hedgehog with long legs.

We all enjoyed the delicious turkey dinner provided by the ladies auxiliary of the church. It was a mighty tired but happy group that fell into bed tonight.

THE HERITAGE BOOK

C<small>OME</small>, ye thankful people, come,
Raise the song of harvest home!
All is safely gathered in,
Ere the winter storms begin:
God, our Maker, doth provide
For our wants to be supplied
Come to God's own temple, come,
Raise the song of harvest home!

—Dean Alford

I HAVE become quite a fan of the Toronto Blue Jays and I follow their games with interest on both radio and television.

I was interested to read that Arthur "Candy" Cummings of Ware, Massachusetts thought up the curveball in 1862 when, as a boy of fourteen, he tossed a clam shell into the ocean and noted its curve. Two years later he found he could duplicate the curve by holding the baseball in a "death grip" and twisting his wrist on release of an underhand pitch.

It may be the curveball that will win the World Series.

TUESDAY — SEPTEMBER 20

MARG and Bruce have had their old bathroom remodelled and replaced the bathtub with a large whirlpool model.

"I am going to be one enormous prune before I get tired of using this tub. The deep water and the bubbles flowing are so relaxing that I could stay in for hours!"

Marg talked me into giving it a try last evening and I found it so enjoyable that I came very close to falling asleep. Those of you who enjoy the luxury of a whirlpool tub in your homes must be sleeping like the proverbial logs.

WEDNESDAY — SEPTEMBER 21

THE autumn frost will lie upon the grass
Like bloom on grapes of purple-brown and
gold.
The misted early mornings will be cold;
The little puddles will be roofed with glass.

With these few lines from Elinor Wylie I welcome autumn today.

THURSDAY — SEPTEMBER 22

THE way to be happy is to make others happy. Helping others is the secret of all success—in business, in the arts, and in the home.

FRIDAY — SEPTEMBER 23

MY mother's influence in molding my character was conspicuous. She forced me to learn daily long chapters of the Bible by heart. To that discipline and patient accurate resolve I owe not only much of my general power of taking pains, but the best of my taste for literature.

—John Ruskin

SATURDAY — SEPTEMBER 24

CHRISTIAN faith is a grand cathedral with divinely pictured windows. Standing without, you can see no glory, nor can imagine any, but standing within every ray of light reveals a harmony of unspeakable splendours.

—Nathaniel Hawthorne

THE HERITAGE BOOK

F OR the whole world before thee is as a little grain of the balance, yea as a drop of the morning dew that falleth down upon the earth. But Thou hast mercy upon all. For Thou lovest all the things that are.

—Wisdom of Solomon 11: 22-24

MONDAY — SEPTEMBER 26

I LOVE squash and tonight's repast was pepper squash stuffed with meat and wild rice. I laughed as I remembered my grandson Marshall's first reaction to this vegetable when he was a small boy.

Margaret had prepared the evening meal, which included squash. Marshall was eating around the squash hoping, I suppose, that it might disappear. Marg insisted that he should at least try it.

Marshall put some in his mouth, chewed courageously, and then swallowed.

About five seconds later he threw up everything he had eaten, and he has not eaten squash from that day to this.

THE HERITAGE BOOK

TUESDAY — SEPTEMBER 27

EVERYONE should keep a fair-sized cemetery in which to bury the faults of their friends.

WEDNESDAY — SEPTEMBER 28

HOPE ever urges us on, and tells us tomorrow will be better.

—*Albuis Tilbullus*

THURSDAY —SEPTEMBER 29

LIFE is the childhood of our immortality.

—*Goethe*

FRIDAY — SEPTEMBER 30

THERE is a beautiful spirit breathing now
Its mellow richness on the clustered trees,
And, from a beaker full of richest dyes,
Pouring new glory on the autumn woods,
And dipping in warm light the pillared
clouds. . . .

—*Henry Wadsworth Longfellow*

October

THE show is over, and the leafy tent
All gold and crimson where the sunlight
   lingered
Through the slow afternoon, is coming down.
The bittersweet is scarlet on the bough
Reluctant to be gone, though frosts have
   strewn
Patins of glory on the forest trails,
While tatters of torn splendour go to feed
The smoky bonfires in the village street.
What singer pipes the closing autumn hush
With surest note of cheer in all the wild?
A dauntless minstrel of the changing year,
Chickadee of the wilderness! He knows
What sweetness gathers in the winter's heart,
What saving oracles the North Wind sings.

—Bliss Carman

THE HERITAGE BOOK

WE plough the fields and scatter
The good seed on the land,
But it is fed and watered
By God's almighty hand:
He sends the snow in winter,
The warmth to swell the grain,
The breezes and the sunshine,
And soft refreshing rain.
All good gifts around us
Are sent from heaven above,
Then thank the Lord, O thank the Lord
For all His love.

—Jane Montgomery Campbell

IT was chilly enough this evening to have our first fire of the autumn season. Last spring my son-in-law Bruce, an exceptionally organized man, cleaned the chimney, fireplace, and hearth thoroughly. Then he carefully laid a fire and declared us prepared for fall.

This evening as I watched the flames flicker and enjoyed the warmth I reflected on the new season's arrival, and my great luck that Marg chose Bruce to be her husband.

THE HERITAGE BOOK

THE autumn sports programs are in full swing at our local high school—football, basketball, volleyball, and cross-country running.

A parent of one of the top cross-country runners told this amusing story.

"Our daughter is an excellent runner and works hard at training. As well as practising with her team at school she puts in many extra hours a week running the country roads near our farm. We worried about her running alone so her father got in the habit of following behind her on his tractor. One day, as I sat on the porch with my parents, Robin came running down the road with Jack right behind her on the tractor.

"'Robin has become a really fast runner,' I said proudly.

"'Heck, I'd be fast too,' said Robin's grandfather, 'if I were being chased by a tractor.'"

THE HERITAGE BOOK

THE colour of the leaves has become magnificent in the past few days. As I walked through the neighbourhood today I found the sight of the trees nearly breathtaking.

Many years ago, when my daughter Mary and her husband John were stationed at a mission overseas, I received a letter from a very homesick young woman. It came at just this time of year.

"Oh Mom, I miss you all so much! Everything here is so hot and dry my teeth feel like they're permanently covered in sand. I keep thinking of our yard and how red the maple leaves on the tree would be. I never knew that I could miss raking leaves so much."

George and I tried to think of a way to help relieve Mary's homesickness. It was George who came up with the solution.

We gathered a huge box of leaves of all kinds and colours and in it we enclosed a child's tiny plastic rake. We sent the box special delivery to Mary and John and the letter we received in return told us that it had been an "absolutely perfect pick-me-up."

THE HERITAGE BOOK

THE worship most acceptable to God comes from a thankful and cheerful heart.

—Plutarch

I REMEMBER when the arrival of autumn meant that we had to face once more the onerous task of the storm windows.

Young people today will never know the dread that those two words could inspire. Today's windows are cleverly fitted into metal tracks, where they slide into place in the fall and then glide smoothly back out of the way in spring.

Real storm windows were fully detachable. The frames were made of wood and they were heavy and unwieldy.

George would stagger up from the basement and then wrestle them into place, often misinterpreting his own markings as to which window went where, which resulted in much muttering and unnecessary hammering.

Cleaning them was another not-to-be-missed joy.

Young people don't know what they've done without—luckily for them.

THE HERITAGE BOOK

AUTUMN is a gypsy
With jewels in her hair.

Autumn is a gypsy
Gay and debonair
Dancing in the sunshine
At the harvest fair,
With confetti whirling
In the golden air.

Autumn is a gypsy
With jewels in her hair.

O MOST merciful Father, who of thy gracious
goodness hast heard the devout prayers of
thy Church, and turned our dearth and
scarcity into cheapness and plenty: We give
thee humble thanks for this thy special bounty:
beseeching thee to continue thy loving-kind-
ness unto us, that our land may yield us her
fruits of increase, to thy glory and comfort:
through Jesus Christ our Lord. Amen.
—Book of Common Prayer for Thanksgiving

THE HERITAGE BOOK

Thanksgiving

As I lay in bed this morning I made a list in my mind of some of the many things I am thankful for. Perhaps you have done the same thing on this special day.

I am thankful for:

My faith,
My health,
My dear friends, near and far,
My home,
My neighbours,
My country,
The beauty of nature around me,
The happiness that I enjoy.

I hope that you too have many reasons to be thankful.

Many of us take the limits of our own field of vision for the limits of the world.

WEDNESDAY — OCTOBER 12

HERE all mankind is equal: rich and poor alike, they love their children.

—Euripides

THURSDAY — OCTOBER 13

WINTER is on its way. I could feel it as I watched the Canada geese fly overhead in their V formations heading south.

The principle of this formation is interesting. Each goose can see where it's going and each goose (except the leader) can see and be seen by at least one other. The older, stronger geese fly in the front of the line to part the air for the ones behind. All the while the birds carry on a constant honking. Perhaps it is a loud farewell to those of us foolish enough to stay in the north for winter.

FRIDAY — OCTOBER 14

THE reason a dog has so many friends is because it wags its tail instead of its tongue.

THE HERITAGE BOOK

IN this autumn season many of my friends and I like to take advantage of the bus tours offered to senior citizens. These "Fall Tours" are many and varied, from one-day trips to the Niagara area to 14-day journeys to the north, east, south or west.

Lila and I chose to join the group heading through upstate New York, Lake Placid, and down to Middlebury, Vermont, returning via Burlington, Vermont up into Quebec and then home along Highway 401.

Today's journey took us through Belleville, Kingston, Brockville, and then Prescott, where we crossed the border into the United States at Ogdensburg. En route, we made several stops at points of historical interest. We lunched at an inn at Gananoque in the Thousand Islands area, and this evening we are staying at the Clarkson Inn in Potsdam, N.Y.

The nicest part of these senior tours is that we meet such a variety of interesting people, most of whom enjoy these slower-paced tours. As well, the tours are very modestly priced, appealing to those of us on fixed incomes.

THE HERITAGE BOOK

WE attended church this morning at the chapel of beautiful St. Laurence University in Canton, New York. It was a joy to see the many young people and to hear their sweet youthful voices singing in this magnificent old church. This verse of one of the morning hymns seemed so appropriate.

Just as I am, young and strong and free
To be the best that I can be,
For truth, and righteousness and Thee
Lord of my life I come.

FOLLOWING the church service yesterday we made the short trip to Lake Placid, New York, site of the Winter Olympics in 1932 and 1980. This is a magnificent area, with beautiful clear lakes surrounded by hills rich in autumn colours.

Several of us went out to see the ski-jump area and took the elevator to the top of the 70-metre jump. It was imposing to say the least. The athletes who use these jumps must be very courageous.

THE HERITAGE BOOK

Tuesday — October 18

THE trip through New York State and into Vermont is studded with American historical landmarks, museums, antique shops, and points of interest to us all.

We enjoyed every minute of the drive and we are resting more than comfortably in The Middlebury Inn.

This inn dates back to 1827 and overlooks the village green. Each room is distinctly decorated and has antique furniture from the Vermont area.

Any of you who happen to be visiting Vermont would enjoy this magnificent old inn.

Wednesday — October 19

To profit from good advice requires more wisdom than to give it.

THE HERITAGE BOOK

IF you have built castles in the air, your work need not be lost; that is where they should be. Now put the foundations under them.

—Henry David Thoreau

I AM not bound to win, but I am bound to be true. I am not bound to succeed, but I am bound to live by the light that I have. I must stand with anybody that stands right, stand with him while he is right, and part with him when he goes wrong.

—Abraham Lincoln

WE are home again after our tour and I feel much richer in many ways.

The scenery viewed, the knowledge gained, and the friendships made make such trips unforgettable.

THE HERITAGE BOOK

SUNDAY — OCTOBER 23

TEACH me to do Thy will: for Thou art my God: Thy spirit is good: lead me into the land of uprightness.

—Psalm 143: 10

MONDAY — OCTOBER 24

No one gets very far unless he accomplishes the impossible at least once a day.

—Elbert Hubbard

TUESDAY — OCTOBER 25

ONLY people who have faith in themselves are able to be faithful to others.

WEDNESDAY — OCTOBER 26

PEOPLE who are difficult to please are often the most worth pleasing.

THE HERITAGE BOOK

Thursday — October 27

A crackling log upon the hearth,
Simmering cider in a mug
A spicy apple red as wine,
A sleepy cat upon the rug;

A great chair with inviting arms
To hold me in its warm embrace,
An ageless book to read once more
And cherish as a dear one's face;

Then let the autumn wind and rain
Come clamoring at my windowpane,
While I, within my citadel,
Am lost beneath enchantment's spell.

—*M. Walton*

Friday — October 28

"Grandpa" Bruce spent this evening with the grandchildren, carving the pumpkins in readiness for Halloween.

Bethany's look of awe as the jack o'lantern was "tested" was worth all the time and effort. A child's happiness is a great reward.

THE HERITAGE BOOK

Saturday — October 29

An unusual amount of common sense is sometimes called wisdom.

Sunday — October 30

For I am persuaded that neither death, nor life, nor angels, nor principalities, nor powers, nor things present, nor things to come, nor height, nor depth, nor any other creature, shall be able to separate us from the love of God, which is in Christ Jesus, our Lord.

—Romans 8: 38-39

Monday — October 31

Today is Halloween and all the little witches and goblins in our neighbourhood have made their way to our door for their treats.

Halloween night is an indicator of neighbourhood change. For several years, as families grew older, we had very few children come to our door. As this generation grew and moved away, new young families have taken their places and tonight we had many little ones "trick or treating" at our door.

November

TODAY is here and mine to use . . .
Tomorrow may not be;
And so the present I would choose
To task my energy.

The opportunity I hold
Within my hand today
May prove to be the precious mould
To shape my future way.

Today is still the only time
In which to do my work,
And mighty triumphs, deeds sublime,
May in its moments lurk.

But even though the lowly vale
Of common life is my way,
The only thing that will avail
Is duty done today.

—*Olive Dunkelburgen*

THE HERITAGE BOOK

WEDNESDAY — NOVEMBER 2

You imagine that I look back on my work with calm and satisfaction. But there is not a single concept of which I am convinced that it will stand firm, and I felt uncertain whether I am in general on the right track. I don't want to be right—I only want to know whether I am right.

—Albert Einstein

THURSDAY — NOVEMBER 3

Will and Muriel gave me a chuckle today.

"You know Edna, I enjoy driving—it gives me a chance to think. I also do some of my best praying while I'm driving," Will said.

In a quiet voice Muriel agreed, "I also do my best praying while you're driving."

FRIDAY — NOVEMBER 4

Only some of us can learn by other people's experiences. Some of us have to be the other people.

SATURDAY — NOVEMBER 5

O NE of the great difficulties that many senior citizens face today is the serious health complication that can result from polypharmacy—the use of multiple medications.

Older people often have multiple ailments with multiple symptoms. Sometimes medications are used to treat symptoms that may be caused by drugs prescribed for another condition.

The family doctor must know about all drugs being taken. Rather than adding a new medication or treatment, withdrawal or modification of the first drug may solve the problem. Doctors must be certain that the patient is getting the most good with the least harm.

Geriatric specialists suggest that patients need to understand why they are on medication. If they are not getting better or are feeling worse the drug medication should be reevaluated.

I guess the very best that we can do is to be aware of the dangers of over-medication and keep our doctors advised of any possible problems.

THE HERITAGE BOOK

DELIGHT thyself also in the Lord; and He shall give thee the desires of thine heart.

—Psalm 37: 4

IT is not by regretting what is irreparable that true work is to be done, but by making the best of what we are. It is not by complaining that we have not the right tools, but by using well the tools we have. What we are and where we are is God's providential arrangement— God's doing, though it may be man's misdoing; and the manly and the wise way is to look your disadvantages in the face and see what can be made out of them. Life, like war, is a series of mistakes, and he is not the best Christian nor the best general who makes the fewest false steps. He is the best who wins the most splendid victories by the retrieval of mistakes. Forget mistakes; organize victory out of mistakes.

—Rev. F. W. Robertson (1816-1853)

TUESDAY — NOVEMBER 8

A FINANCIAL genius is someone who can earn money faster than his or her family can spend it.

WEDNESDAY — NOVEMBER 9

F ROM my mother came the idea that going down to the sea repaired the spirit. That is where she walked when she was sad or worried or lonely for my father. If she had been crying, she came back composed; if she had left angry with us, she returned in good humour. So we naturally believed that there was a cleansing, purifying effect to be had; that letting the fresh wind blow through your mind and spirits, as well as your hair and clothing, purged black thoughts; that contemplating the ceaseless motion of the waves calmed a raging spirit.

—*Robert MacNeil*

THURSDAY — NOVEMBER 10

P EOPLE show what they are by what they do with what they have.

THE HERITAGE BOOK

Remembrance Day

Never again down the quiet street
Will his eager footsteps hurrying ring;
Never again will he whistle a tune,
Or boist'rously raise his voice to sing.
The little park lies over the way,
And the big tree stands, where he carved his
    name;
And everything looks unchanged to me
Yet strangely, heartbreakingly, not the same.

. . . Dear he was to his mother's heart,
Big and generous, good and kind;
Now he is lying in foreign soil,
And all that he loved is left behind.

Mourn not overmuch. Britain called,
And you gave your best, your little son.
As long as the empire's records stand
His name is there, and the deeds he's done
Nothing is wasted—time, nor love,
Nor the weary days that stretch ahead.
Britain called in her direst need—
Proudly you gave her your precious dead.

—Ann Ryan

THE HERITAGE BOOK

I HAVE always enjoyed reading or hearing about those clever ideas that make homemaking just a little easier. Here are just a few of my "hints that help"—collected over many years.

• Wipe a drop of vinegar over each eyeglass lens to shine it clean and streak-free.

• Charcoal in a toolbox will keep tools from rusting.

• Potatoes won't sprout in storage if an apple is placed among them.

• Cut an "X" in the stems of broccoli, cauliflower, or Brussels sprouts so that they will cook in half the usual time.

• Mould on jelly doesn't penetrate below the surface so remove visible mould and what remains is edible.

• Rub butter over the cut side of an onion to keep it fresh for future use.

• A piece of celery in the bread bag will keep the bread fresh.

THE HERITAGE BOOK

I WILL give thanks to the Lord with all my heart; I will tell of all thy wonders. I will be glad and exult in Thee; I will sing praise to Thy name, O Most High.

—Psalm 9: 1-2

N O man, for any considerable time, can wear one face to himself and another to the multitude without finally getting bewildered as to which may be the true.

—Nathaniel Hawthorne

S TRUGGLE diligently against your impatience, and strive to be amiable and gentle, in season and out of season, towards every one, however much they may vex and annoy you, and be sure God will bless your efforts.

—St. Francis de Sales

THE HERITAGE BOOK

My good friend Mavis is planning a family reunion for next summer. She comes from a large family, many of whom are scattered all across Canada and the United States, so it is quite a task. Mavis offers these tips to those of you who may wish to hold a gathering for your own family.

• Give yourself plenty of time. Eight to ten months seems to be a typical time frame for organizing.

• Don't try to do everything by yourself. Delegate, form committees, and allow them to do their jobs. Involve all generations of your family in the planning and preparations.

• A newsletter can be very useful. It keeps people informed of plans and you may solicit ideas and volunteers.

• Photo albums, slides, and videos are an important part of any reunion. Ask everyone to contribute and set aside time for viewing.

• Photocopied sheets of the names, addresses, and phone numbers of all those attending is a nice touch.

• Some lasting memento of the occasion is always appreciated.

THE HERITAGE BOOK

THURSDAY — NOVEMBER 17

COME friend, my fire is burning bright
A fire's no longer out of place,
How clear it glows! (there's frost tonight)
It looks white winter in the face.
                                    —*Thomas Constable*

FRIDAY — NOVEMBER 18

ONE advantage of marriage is that when you fall out of love with him, or he falls out of love with you, it keeps you together until you fall in again.

                                    —*Judith Viorst*

SATURDAY — NOVEMBER 19

WE all have something to give. So if you know how to read, find someone who can't. If you've got a hammer, find a nail. If you're not hungry, not lonely, not in trouble—seek out someone who is.

                                    —*George Bush in a State of the Union Address*

THE HERITAGE BOOK

REJOICE always; pray without ceasing; in everything give thanks; for this is God's will for you in Christ Jesus.

—1 Thessalonians 5: 16-18

IN times of crisis we must avoid both ignorant change and ignorant opposition to change.

ON this date in 1963, in Dallas, Texas, President John F. Kennedy was assassinated. During the one thousand days that he spent in office, he brought to his country a sense of optimism and a new sense of working together for the good of all.

"Let the word go forth from this time and place to friend and foe alike, that the torch has been passed to a new generation of Americans—born in this century, tempered by war, disciplined by a hard and bitter peace."

THE HERITAGE BOOK

Novemeber is a dreary month. I hope this recipe for Harvest Soup will brighten your day.

1/4 cup of butter
1 large onion, chopped
2 leeks (white part only) chopped
1 large potato peeled, diced
1 cup thinly sliced carrots
2 cups diced squash (small cubes)
3 cups chicken stock
1 1/2 cups light cream
salt, pepper
Garnish: chopped chives, sour cream, and grated carrot.

In a large, heavy pot, melt butter and cook onions and leeks until softened, but not browned. Stir in potato, carrots and squash. Cook, stirring for 2 to 3 minutes. Pour in stock, cover and simmer for about 20 minutes or until vegetables are tender.

Purée in blender or food processor until very smooth. Return to saucepan. Stir in cream to desired consistency. Heat until hot but do not boil. Season with salt and pepper to taste, then add garnish. Serves six.

Thursday — November 24

As I walked past the mirror in the hall today, I looked at myself and I was startled to see an old woman looking back at me. It probably sounds silly to you but I don't think of myself as old.

You see, inside I am still the young woman who married George McCann and left home as the wife of a recently ordained minister. In my mind I still dance and sing and read stories to my young daughters. I can run with the wind in my hair and I can skate waltzes with my husband on the pond.

Sometimes I wish that my grandchildren and great-grandchildren could have known me as I was then.

Maybe it's enough that I remember.

Friday — November 25

Prayer should be the key of the day and the lock of the night.

THE HERITAGE BOOK

SATURDAY — NOVEMBER 26

IT is much more difficult to judge oneself than to judge others.

—Antoine de Saint Exupery

SUNDAY — NOVEMBER 27

Advent Sunday

BUT the salvation of the righteous is from the Lord. He is their strength in time of trouble. And the Lord helps them, and delivers them; He delivers them from the wicked, and saves them, because they take refuge in Him.

—Psalm 37: 39-40

MONDAY — NOVEMBER 28

WE love old cathedrals, old furniture, old silver, old dictionaries and old prints, but we have entirely forgotten about the beauty of old men. I think an appreciation of that kind of beauty is essential to our life; for beauty, it seems to me, is what is old and mellow and well smoked.

—Lin Yutang

THE HERITAGE BOOK

A GE is a high price to pay for maturity.

THAN these November skies
Is no sky lovelier. The clouds are deep;
Into their grey the subtle spies
Of colour creep,
Changing that high austerity to delight,
Till ev'n the leaden interfold are bright.
And, where the clouds break, faint far azure
    peers
Ere a thin flushing cloud again
Shuts up that loveliness, or shares.
The huge great clouds move slowly, gently as
Reluctant the quick sun should shine in vain,
Holding in bright caprice their rain,
And when of colours none,
Nor rose, nor amber, nor the scarce late
    green,
Is truly seen—
In all the myriad grey,
In silver height and dusky deep, remain
The loveliest,
Faint purple flushes of the unvanquished sun.
                    —*John Freeman (1881-1929)*

December

Success

I HOLD no dream of fortune vast,
Nor seek undying fame,
I do not ask when life is past
That many know my name.

I may not own the skill to rise
To glory's topmost height,
Nor win a place among the wise,
But I can keep the right.

And I can live my life on earth
Contented to the end,
If but a few shall know my worth
And proudly call me friend.

—Edgar Guest

THE HERITAGE BOOK

Friday — December 2

Tradition is what was once a bright new idea.

Saturday — December 3

Our church choir began practising today for the Christmas musical presentation. Phyllis, who has a beautiful voice, gave us a brief hint of what we will hear when she came singing through the door to pick up the twins after her practice.

I remember well that as a minister's wife I was expected to sing in the choir. I was designated as a soprano, although many of my high notes sounded like a squeaky gate. I got in the habit of practising high notes whenever I walked alone in open spaces, always quitting if anyone approached.

One day a car, windows open, sneaked up on me at an intersection just as I was reaching for some of my more difficult notes.

The startled young man who was driving quickly pulled over to the curb, jumped out and checked under the hood of his car.

Mortified, I walked on—in silence.

THE HERITAGE BOOK

SUNDAY — DECEMBER 4

Second Sunday in Advent

BLESSED Lord, who has caused all holy
Scriptures to be written for our learning;
Grant that we may in such wise hear them,
read, mark, learn and inwardly digest them,
that by patience and comfort of thy holy Word,
we may embrace and ever hold fast the blessed
hope of everlasting life, which thou has given
us in our Saviour, Jesus Christ. Amen.

—The Book of Common Prayer

MONDAY — DECEMBER 5

A CERTAIN friction between the generations is
inevitable. That's because the young and
the old have all the answers, and those in between are stuck with the questions.

TUESDAY — DECEMBER 6

TACT is the ability to laugh at your own stories—no matter who tells them.

THE HERITAGE BOOK

Any Little Old Song

ANY little old song
Will do for me,
Tell it of joys gone long,
    Or joys to be,
Or friendly faces best
    Loved to see.
Newest themes I want not
    On subtle strings,
And for thrillings pant not
    That new song brings:
I only need the homeliest
    Of heart-stirrings.

—Thomas Hardy

THURSDAY — DECEMBER 8

MARG and I enjoyed this afternoon at our local school. We were involved in the "Christmas Craft Day"—a school-wide project that allows the children to make the Christmas decoration of their choice.

Marg worked in the kitchen with a group of youngsters who made bread dough Santas, which they painted and made into refrigerator magnets.

I worked in a classroom where a father helped students cut out wooden ornaments with a jigsaw. I mixed paint so that the children could paint and later shellac their creations.

With the help of many volunteers the craft day was a huge success. I hope each child has been given a happy memory of Christmas for 1994.

FRIDAY — DECEMBER 9

A BIG person is not one who makes no mistakes, but one who is bigger than any mistakes he or she makes.

THE HERITAGE BOOK

SATURDAY — DECEMBER 10

My dear friend and neighbour Lila MacGuiness lives on her own, but depends on friends to help her with the daily chores that her health does not permit her to do.

Marg and I have decided to make Lila a number of meals that can be frozen and then heated in the microwave—sort of a homemade T.V. dinner.

I hope Lila will get as much pleasure in eating the dinners as we will in making them.

SUNDAY — DECEMBER 11

The Advent of our King
Our prayers must now employ
And we must hymns of welcome sing
In strains of holy joy.
—*Reverend John Chandler*

MONDAY — DECEMBER 12

Do not resent growing old; many are denied that privilege.

TUESDAY — DECEMBER 13

IF you think you have someone eating out of your hand, it's a good idea to count your fingers.

WEDNESDAY — DECEMBER 14

AT whatever age, I hope to die young.

—*Jean LeMoyne*

THURSDAY — DECEMBER 15

ADVICE is like snow—the softer it falls, the longer it dwells upon and the deeper it sinks into the mind.

—*Coleridge*

FRIDAY — DECEMBER 16

A GOOD slogan for a happy home life is the old railroad cross-warning sign: "Stop, Look and Listen."

THE HERITAGE BOOK

IF I had to live my life over again, I'd dare to make more mistakes next time. . . .

I would take more trips. I would climb more mountains, swim more rivers. I would eat more ice cream and less beans.

I would perhaps have more actual troubles, but I'd have fewer imaginary ones. You see I'm one of those people who live seriously and sanely, hour after hour, day after day.

Oh I've had my moments. And if I had it to do over again, I'd have more of them.

In fact I'd try to have nothing else, just moments, one after another, instead of living so many years ahead of each day. . . .

If I had to live my life over, I would start barefoot earlier in the spring and stay that way later in the fall.

I would go to more dances.

I would ride more merry-go-rounds.

I would pick more daisies.

—Nadine Stair in her 85th year

THE HERITAGE BOOK

WE long to hear Thy voice,
To see Thee face to face,
To share Thy crown and glory then,
As now we share Thy grace.
Come Lord, and wipe away
The curse, the sin, the strain;
And make this blighted world of ours
Thine own fair world again.

—Rev. H. Bonar

MY friend Betty, who has been confined for many years, explained to me, "You know, Edna, this time of year is especially difficult for those of us who are unable to get out. You have no idea how much it means when friends or neighbours stop in to tell us about their shopping trips or the decorations up in the malls. It enables us to enjoy, vicariously, the excitement of the season."

As Christmas Day draws near I like to remind my readers that this is an important time of year to remember our friends who are shut-ins.

TUESDAY — DECEMBER 20

Do not follow where the path may lead. Go instead where there is no path and leave a trail.

WEDNESDAY — DECEMBER 21

An old man, having retired from active life, regains the gaiety and irresponsibility of childhood. He is ready to play. . . . He cannot run with his son, but he can totter with his grandson. Our first and last steps have the same rhythm.

—André Maurois

THURSDAY — DECEMBER 22

"A babe in a house is a wellspring of pleasure, a messenger of peace and love, a resting place for innocence on earth, a link between angels and men."

These words by Martin Tupper seemed especially appropriate as we get ready to celebrate the birth of the "blessed Babe" in the lowly manger so long ago.

FRIDAY — DECEMBER 23

ON Christmas Eve our family attends the 7 p.m. family service at our church and then returns home with friends for a late buffet dinner and carol sing. Even when family members are unable to be with us there is always a phone call at about nine o'clock: "I just had to call! I knew you'd all be there."

Someone once said, "Rituals reveal what a family stands for. They are its essence, distilled into acts that imprint the family's values on its members."

"In our family we always . . ." gives every member a feeling of belonging and the joy of shared memories.

SATURDAY — DECEMBER 24

I LOVE all the children who sleep on Christmas Eve
With dreams of Christmas morning, who in
    these dreams believe;
For children are God's classics, yet meek and
    small and mild
And fashioned also by His hand like the
    blessed small Christ-child.

—Nellie Varnes Fultz

THE HERITAGE BOOK

SUNDAY — DECEMBER 25

AND the angel said to them, "Do not be afraid; for behold, I bring you good news of a great joy which shall be for all the people; for today in the city of David, there has been born for you a Saviour who is Christ the Lord. And this will be a sign for you; you will find a baby wrapped in cloths, and lying in a manger."

—Luke 2: 10-12

MONDAY — DECEMBER 26

ANGELS from the realms of glory,
Wing your flight o'er all the earth;
Ye who sang creation's story,
Now proclaim Messiah's birth;
Come and worship
Worship Christ the new-born King.

—James Montgomery

TUESDAY — DECEMBER 27

WHAT is good enough for "company" is not too good for your family, be it courtesy or the silver tea-pot.

—Emily Murphy

WEDNESDAY — DECEMBER 28

As the year comes to a close, I try to take some time to reflect on both the year that has passed and on the new year that is arriving. ("What have I accomplished? What shall I do this year to make it better than the one just ended?")

Ralph Waldo Emerson said, "This time, like all other times, is a very good one, if we but know what to do with it."

THURSDAY — DECEMBER 29

In the deep, unwritten wisdom of life there are many things to be learned that cannot be taught. We never know them by hearing them spoken, but we grow into them by experience and recognize them through understanding. Understanding is a great experience in itself, but it does not come through instruction.

—Anthony Hope

FRIDAY — DECEMBER 30

Faith is believing in things when common sense tells you not to.

THE HERITAGE BOOK

THIS is the time of endings,
but of new beginnings, too . . .

God sends us another year
and maketh all things new . . .

Another hope, another chance,
another road to take . . .

Another star to follow,
and another start to make . . .

New beginnings, new adventures,
new heights to attain . . .

Golden opportunities
to work and build again . . .

New and higher aspiration,
for the future days . . .

Seeking, dreaming, moving on
down bright and better ways.

—Patience Strong

HAPPY NEW YEAR!

Best wishes
Alice De Graaf

Get well soon
Carole Udell

Best wishes
Laurie Smith